American Wood Heat Cookery

SECOND EDITION, REVISED AND ENLARGED

by Margaret Byrd Adams

with Donna Nagely

To my kindling — Maya and Jessica

MarrasM Press, 22 Reynolds Street
  Alfred, New York 14802
© 1998 by Margaret Byrd Adams Rasmussen. All rights reserved
Printed in the United States of America

First edition published in 1981
Second edition published in 1984
Second edition reprinted in 1998

Edited by Betsy Rupp Fulwiler
Designed by Judy Petry

Cover photograph by Fred Milkie, courtesy of Sutter Home
  Woodstoves Inc., Seattle

Library of Congress Cataloging in Publication Data
Main entry under title:

American wood heat cookery.

   Rev. ed. of: Warm & tasty. c1981.
   Index includes.
   1. Cookery, American. 2. Stoves, Wood. I. Adams,
Margaret Byrd, 1942-   .II. Warm & tasty.
TX715.W279 1984   641.5 '8   84-7633
ISBN 0-914718-91-6

Contents

Introduction	7
The Stove Story	9
Heat Stove Cookery	14
Recipes	27
Soups and Beverages	28
Side Dishes	56
Main Dishes	72
Breads and Such	135
Sweets	153
Stove-Top Parties	192
Stove Care	233
Ten Wood Tips	235
Heat Value of Woods	236
Safe Temperatures of Meat and Poultry	238

This book exists because of—
Yvonne Michie Horn;
Donna Nagely, who worked in the initial stages of this book as researcher, friend, and moral supporter with excellent standards that earmark this book;
my family, especially my mother and children;
all the incredible people who kept my kids, reacted to and corrected copy, tasted and tested recipes, and wouldn't let me give up;
my librarians: David Campbell, Carolyn ApRoberts, Mary Mason, Kerry Arkell, and Ruth Ann Edwards;
Holly Schmidt, who read every rough word;
historians and researchers across the country who answered my pleas for historical recipes.

Introduction

Americans banished wood heating stoves to dusty basements and garages fifty years ago. Now world politics and a fossil fuel shortage have brought them back with dignity. With them have come some pleasure and frugality to American households.

Wood heating sends us back to forests to gather wood. It stretches our dormant wood-chopping muscles and keeps us physically fit. It revives family life as we shrink into one-room living for the first time since furnaces spread us all through the house. It heats our homes for a fraction of our former fuel bills. And there's one more thing—we can cook on wood heat stoves!

Wood heat stove cookery—not to be confused with kitchen wood stove cookery—doubles the value of the wood pile. It turns cheap meats and tough vegetables into exotic dishes.

With the wood stove revival, we return the culture of cooking to the family hearth of yesteryear. Our American heritage of heating and eating dates back to the native Indians and colonial housewives who stirred stews over the same fire that heated the dwelling. The idea of a separate cooking unit in a separate room of the house—isolated from family activity—is a modern phenomenon. When you already heat your home with a wood stove, why should you shiver off to a cold kitchen and use a second energy source? You can put dinner on the heat stove to cook itself and curl up with a good book or visit with your family.

No matter what style stove you own—a highly efficient air limited, an antique restoration or reproduction, or a homemade creation—you can cook on it. That may mean on the top, in the firebox, or over an open pot hole, depending on your model.

Do not exclude heat stove cooking because you heat with coal or corncobs instead of wood. You can use any procedures in this book to suit the fuel in your heater.

Cooking on the heater makes a few special demands. It is a patient art—not a science—of experimentation and improvisation. You will have to give up knob turning and button pushing and prepare yourself to cook by the way food looks and not by time and temperature.

By its very nature, wood cooking tenderizes and preserves flavor in foods with the slow, simmer heat. My father talked all his life of the sweet potatoes he carried to school in his trousers' pocket when he was a boy in Edgefield, South Carolina. The potato kept him warm on the way and when he got there, the creamy, flavorful vegetable warmed his stomach at lunchtime. It was a taste that he cherished and one he feared was gone with the original wood stove era. As we reclaim wood heat, we reclaim ash-baked sweet potatoes and create our own tales to tell our children.

We have lost a lot of the culture and expertise of living with a wood stove, our most authentic American home symbol. It's time to fill the gap.

American Wood Heat Cookery is like the old-fashioned cookery books that entertained in fine prose and were total household manuals with recipes. *American Wood Heat Cookery* entertains with the history of the wood stove and the heritage of America through the food on the table. It is a total manual of wood stove operation that helps you enjoy the culture of wood stoves in the present day.

American Wood Heat Cookery is also a modern cookbook. Recipes are written in precise quantities rather than in "smidgens," "handfuls," and "pinches." Detailed instructions are given without destroying your imagination or the atmosphere of wood cookery.

The recipes in this book came from wood stove and fireplace cooks around America. They bequeath to us the taste of foreign lands whose emigrants came to America, the pioneer spirit that pushed our ancestors across the plains, political rallies and cowpoke campfires, and Grandmother's Sunday dinners.

"The intention of every other piece of prose may be discussed and even mistrusted," said Joseph Conrad, "but the purpose of a cookery book is one and unmistakable. Its object can conceivably be no other than to increase the happiness of mankind."

The Stove Story

The Arab oil embargo of 1973 made chopping wood a glamorous alternative to paying the fuel bills. Only a million people heated with wood in America ten years ago, and they kept it quiet around their neighbors who used gas, oil, and electricity. But by 1980 six million "oil-burned" Americans had created a "Wood Heat Stove Revival."

Indeed, it was a fuel shortage in the eighteenth century that made it possible to choose from a sophisticated range of stove designs today. When wood was too scarce to meet both domestic and industrial demands in the glass and iron producing regions of Germany, Frederick the Great took action. He held a contest to find a stove design that would give more heat for less wood than the current models did. Such a domestic stove freed up fuel for industry. Rulers of Denmark, Norway, and Sweden had the same problem and held similar competitions. The results of these contests are the stoves we see with sylvan scenes raised on their sides to radiate more heat and the fuel efficient, air limited stoves with well-designed baffle and draft systems.

As European leaders rewarded stove improvement, Americans kept cooking and heating in the huge open fireplaces that dominated their homes. The first wood stove produced in the United States in Lynn, Massachusetts, in 1642 caused little stir and was not appealing enough to pull cooks away from their familiar hearths.

But around 1744, a wood shortage in Philadelphia inspired Benjamin Franklin to improve on the fireplace. He had seen the European stoves in his world travels and studied the small stoves that German settlers brought with them to Pennsylvania. He quipped that the Germans would "probably take over the country from the English." It was embarrassingly obvious that the Germans' wood piles diminished more slowly than their English neighbors'.

Franklin invented a three-sided metal affair that protruded into the room and provided a top surface for cooking. This open stove took one-fourth the fuel to raise the room temperature twice as high, and Franklin could even prepare his daily cup of medicinal chocolate on the "iron fireplace." This is the first reference to anyone cooking on a stove top. The best anyone had done until then was to place an iron slab on legs over the fire to hold pots and pans.

Franklin had an all-American idea—more heat plus a cooking surface, without giving up the view of the fire. Because he refused to patent his invention for profit—in his usual statesmanlike manner—other inventors continued to develop his idea. It does not seem to have hurt

Ben's fame. Today's Franklin fireplace—although a far cry from his version—has continued to be a popular heating unit. And after all, have you ever heard of a Rumford fireplace?

Probably not, although Count Rumford, born Benjamin Thomas, was an American-born experimenter whose stove is significant in stove development. He designed a stove in the late 1700s based on his belief that a fire "contained in as small a space as possible provided the most efficient type of cooking." It was a boxlike stove much like Franklin's. But he made a bigger fuss about cooking on it than Ben did. At last, after years of bending over a smoky fire, cooks could stand up to cook. They were so delighted they did not even lament the lack of an oven—a luxury for many cooks even into the twentieth century.

Almost a hundred years after Franklin's stove was developed, women still could not finish ironing three shirts before they had to stop and stuff a log in the stove to keep the soup simmering. In 1836, one Isaac Orr in Washington, D. C., patented the first "airtight" stove. His tightly jointed stove of sheet iron with air drafts was the first American attempt to control burning in the stove. Stoves were indeed improving.

A stove was designed specifically for cooking in 1845. It raised the surface of the stove to waist level and provided a good-sized cooking space. In addition, the stove had a hole in the top (with a removable lid) in which to set a kettle. Henry Miller in Worcester, Massachusetts, added a second hole later on and even put a little box in his stove so women could bake bread.

Once women had a taste of stove cooking, they would not settle for less. The ones who made it to the end of the Oregon Trail did not wait long before they had the luxury they had left behind. The first iron stove was cast in Oregon about the same time the last wagon trains had come overland. "No small number of curiosity seekers" came to view the stove that caused a minor sensation at Ladd and Tilton Bank on Front Street in Portland. Iron ore had been discovered in the Oswego Hills upriver and the new town there was expected to become the "Pittsburgh of the West." Considerable iron was processed—and stoves produced—but alas, plagues of business mismanagement left Lake Oswego to develop into a peaceful Portland suburb.

When America became industrialized and Americans got richer, stoves became more sophisticated. Parlor stoves gleamed with chrome and isinglass and the kettle and soup pot holes hid under chrome lids. Wood kitchen ranges with warming ovens and baking ovens and even thermometers on their doors were shiny and polished with porcelain finishes touched with chrome.

The laundry stove is a fossil in the evolution of stoves and worthy of note. A short, squat stove on legs, it had a square top with two or four pot holes that could be removed to hold a griddle for cooking. The stove had a hot water reservoir attached for heating the wash water. On laundry day, these stoves were fired up and kept blazing all day. A pot of soup or beans simmered on the back corner and was ready when the wash was finished. It was a functional, all-purpose unit that was one of the last of the wood stoves to go.

At the peak of the original wood stove era in the first half of the twentieth century, forty million American homes were heated with wood stoves. Some people had kitchen ranges, but many continued to have only one heating and cooking source. As our economy developed, stoves developed, too. The wood stove era waned and people found other ways to heat their houses—with furnaces and electric room units. Coin-operated propane stoves (drop a quarter in and cook your dinner) and oil heaters were replaced by electric stoves for cooking when electricity became popular around 1930. Heating with wood was such a stigma that some stove companies designed a circulating wood heater to look like an oil burner so their customers wouldn't be embarrassed in front of their more affluent neighbors.

The array of stoves both new and antique on the market today is evidence that Americans are taking pride in their wood piles and their new heating systems. The collection of stoves—cast-iron, sheet steel, tile, porcelain, air limited (sometimes called airtight), thermostat controlled, manually controlled, fire-brick lined models—would so stagger Frederick the Great that he probably could not decide who deserved the prize. Stoves available in the wood stove revival have made major strides in design. They are cleaner and fit more easily into our sterile homes than the old models. Draft controls and manual or automatic thermostats further suit them to modern living.

Cookware

Cooking utensils have evolved along with stoves. (Many modern kitchen utensils not originally designed for wood stove use can be adapted to wood cookery.) But the utensils that originated with wood stoves continue to serve well.

Cast iron has been appreciated for its cooking qualities—it absorbs heat, spreads it evenly, and retains it—since man learned to refine iron ore over four thousand years ago. In the sixteenth century pots were bulbous forms that narrowed at the rim and then flared out. Kettles, or boiling vessels, widened at the rim. These utensils, cast in two parts, are easily identified by a vertical seam down the side.

Americans began to cast iron pots in 1650. In the 1830s and 1840s when iron pots moved to the stove, they did not have to do heavy duty over an open fire so they became thin walled and lighter weight. By 1870 the pot designs were refined and simplified for easier mass production. Bottoms tapered to fit into pot holes. Pots lost their legs. Spiders—three-legged skillets—had their legs sawed off and were later made legless.

Noted American chef James Beard compares the most recent innovation of modern smooth surface cooking stoves to the perfection of the "iron age kitchen" in which people cooked on cast-iron stoves with cast-iron pots. The flat stove surface dispersed the heat well and cooks slid pots over the top from low heat ("back-of-the-stove") to higher heat over the stove's "hot spot," the place on the stove directly over the fire or hot draft.

Manufacturers never stopped producing cast-iron cookware. The Griswold Company was founded in 1865 and has continued to be the oldest existing brand name in cookware. Cast-iron pans baked corn bread in the shape of corn sticks and muffins as hearts and diamonds. Waffle irons and griddles fitted right on the stove top, unlike the electric plug-ins we have known since the late thirties. The Dutch oven, a large pot with a flat

lid, spent the gap between wood stove eras on campfires and is perhaps the only other utensil besides the skillet that did not go into hiding during the wood stove gap.

In addition to cast iron, we have imported copper utensils since colonial times. But even in those days they were affordable only by the wealthy. A copper foundry in Lynn, Massachusetts, produced copper kettles as early as 1660. Today it is imported from Europe for gourmet cooks who prize it because it spreads heat evenly and quickly and loses heat quickly. It works well on the wood stove and cooks food faster than cast iron does.

Speckled graniteware has stayed on the market from olden wood stove days because it was used for camp cooking and was inexpensive. But few original antique pieces are still usable because the lightweight cookware chips and loses its surface. The impatient cook preferred this faster cooking utensil to cast iron. And it was also less expensive.

Fire and Ashes

Early wood stove users took every possible precaution to avoid the cry of "Fire," which usually meant a family would be left homeless. In colonial days men stopped their work and grabbed buckets to form a line from the fire to the town well. Usually their best efforts were futile.

Clean chimneys were the major fire insurance they had. Creosote—the sticky tar that collects inside the chimney from improper draft and incomplete burning of green or wet wood—catches fire easily. Chimney sweeps operated in North America during the earlier stove age to control the fire hazard. They can be seen today with their stovepipe hats and flapping coattails. In Europe, sweeps read chimneys like our electric man reads meters. They check you on a regular schedule, depending on your creosote buildup patterns, and trouble you only for the fee. One ancient chimney cleaning method suggested by a savvy European to a novice new-stove burner in America was to lower an energetic young goose down the chimney on a rope and let it flap the creosote away. Or after Christmas, you can pull the Yule tree up and down the chimney.

Finally, the story of stoves includes ashes, which once were vital in household ecology. Left in the bottom of a stove, they prolonged its life. Old-timers made soap from the lye that leached out of the ashes and from grease and fat from cooking. They even rinsed dinner plates into a resevoir with hot water to collect every bit of fat that solidified on the water. Our forebears also used ashes in the garden to control pests and as fertilizer. (Hardwood ashes used for cooking fires are especially good soil improvers.) They sprinkled them on icy paths in wintertime to prevent falls and threw them on garbage heaps to discourage rats and mice.

Heat Stove Cookery

Now that you have decided to cook on your wood stove, be prepared to innovate and improvise. Wood stove cooks—past and present—offer suggestions and hints to start you off.

What to cook? Try anything. Suit the day's menu to the weather outside—if it is snowy, you will have a hotter fire and can bake cakes and stir-fry dishes that require more heat. If it is only chilly outside, you will do best to simmer soups, stews, and casseroles and fix dishes that need a simmering heat. (After you become a wood stove cook, you will never again want to push "high" on your conventional range.) Chicken, beef, pork, fish, vegetables, and grains all take kindly to this method. Steamed breads and puddings are perfect for the wood stove top; they originated there. Quick cooking foods such as omelets and pastas turn out more nutritional and better textured than when cooked over electric or gas heat. Delicate sauces that require gentle temperatures to melt butter and cheeses seldom fail. Breads and cakes usually cooked in absolute degrees in your conventional oven also can be baked on the stove top.

The rule of thumb is to make wood stove cookery easy for yourself and make it fit your life-style—not change your life-style to fit your new venture. If you work, you can cook meals a day ahead and have dinner waiting when you get home the next day. Cooking a day ahead works well for soups because you can cool them and skim unwanted fat off the top before reheating them to eat. It works equally well with potatoes that need to cook and cool for salads, or any dishes that improve their flavor by sitting a day. If you tend the home fires, you can bake, stew, and stir all day with no limitations.

Wondering how to take the kitchen into the parlor? Do messy preparations in the kitchen ahead of time and bring them into the family room on a tray or rolling cart. Work up a tray of basic tools, utensils, and staples to keep by the stove, especially if your kitchen is on another floor of the house or too many steps away from the family room. Women on the Oregon Trail hustled up meals as soon as the wagon wheels stopped rolling because they had everything handy in the "grub box" attached to the side of the covered wagon. Everything was right at hand—a Dutch oven, kettle, frying pan, coffee pot, rolling pin, bread pan, milk can, and eating utensils.

You also can use the chafing dish idea that originated in the late 1800s when women were already getting tired of being in the kitchen away from guests and family. A few of the more liberated women gathered all the dinner dish ingredients on a tray and took it into the parlor. There they cooked it in a pot suspended on a rack over an open flame. The wood stove top replaces the flame and liberates you from the kitchen. You will enjoy giving parties when the wood stove cooks the dishes and serves as a buffet. You will feel like a guest, too. Cook the food and then raise the dishes onto trivets to stay warm through the party. And don't worry about messing up your stove top. There are ways to clean it (see "Stove Care").

Know Your Stove

Get to know your stove. How can it be used for cooking? Do you have easy access to the firebox so you can cook in the ashes? Is the top surface large enough for your pots and pans? How many will it hold? Do you have a removable lid on the stove top to allow broiling and direct heat between flame and pot bottom? Where is the hot spot? Where is the low heat area? How hot does the surface get?

Your answers depend on the kind of stove you own. For cooking purposes, we separate stoves into three categories: (1) cast-iron antique design, non-air limited; (2) foreign and domestic cast iron, air limited; and (3) domestic sheet steel, air limited.

Cast-iron models, air limited or less fuel efficient, have complete cooking possibilities. The flat metal surface spreads heat and holds it. Often it has pot holes with removable lids. Sometimes you can insert griddles and waffle irons into the holes. If you do not mind scrubbing sooty pot bottoms, you can remove the pot hole lids and cook directly over the flames. Or you can broil over the open hole.

Foreign and domestic air limited stoves are very fuel efficient and hold a steady heat for cooking. They have draft systems that can be manipulated to get the cooking surface temperature you need. They also often have a removable pot hole lid and a firebox with easy access.

Domestic airtights, or air limiteds, of sheet steel have a flat surface or sometimes a tiered surface that makes two convenient levels of cooking heat. The flat, sheet steel stove surfaces radiate a higher heat than you suspect—as high as 700 degrees Fahrenheit. (One cook told me her stove was not hot enough for cooking. When I persuaded her to try it she burned her English muffins.)

Utensils

Start in your own kitchen to collect a basic inventory of utensils—skillets, saucepans, casseroles with lids, baking pans, roasting pan, stockpot, vegetable steamer, steamer kettle, wire racks, Dutch oven, trivets, tongs. Then spread out to hardware stores, antique and thrift shops, garage sales, and kitchen supply houses as your enthusiasm and pocketbook allow. You can buy new cast-iron pieces from the same manufacturers who sold them to

your grandmother and collect griddles, waffle irons, stove top toasters—whatever suits your stove. If you want to collect old cast-iron cookware, avoid pitted or cracked pieces. They are best used for planting geraniums.

Cookware Materials

The best pots have flat bottoms and straight sides and are made of metals that diffuse and conduct heat readily. Handles can be nonmetal or metal. Choose utensils of materials from the past—cast iron, speckled graniteware, copper—or from the modern age—heavy aluminum, stainless steel, tin, foil, or Pyrex. If you live in a mild climate, lightweight utensils work better than cast iron, which needs more heat to do the cooking.

Foil is a modern marvel that found its way into American kitchens in the forties and has affected every aspect of food preparation, including cleanup. It conducts heat but does not retain it and has no flavor to transmit to the food. Old wood stove cooks surely would envy us because we can use it to wrap foods for cooking and seal moisture into steamed puddings, and never have to wash it.

Heavy aluminum cookware thoroughly diffuses heat and so is excellent for griddles and in cooking casseroles and stews. It may cloud sauces and stocks, so some cooks avoid it. Stainless steel is another metal our great grandmothers missed out on. It caused such a revolution in the kitchen that Emily Post changed American table manners. She made it proper to cut your salad with your knife because oil and vinegar on the salad did not discolor the knife and cause the hostess extra work to scour it.

While stainless steel is perhaps the easiest cookware to maintain, cast iron requires some special attention as it has to be seasoned. But once you season it and care for it properly, it will be problem-free, too. (New cast iron is sometimes preseasoned at the factory.) Seasoning is a minor art: Remove any rust with steel wool, rub a thin coating of grease or oil on the utensil, then put it on the stove top for about thirty minutes. Repeat this as many times as you wish. Ten or more is not too much to get a nonstick surface.

To clean cast iron, just wipe it with a rag. If food has hardened on it, put a small amount of water in it and put it on the stove. Steam it and then dry it. Some people never submerge their cast iron in water. Some rub it clean with salt. You may wish to keep a separate pot for fish and use other pans for other foods.

Never leave any unwatched empty pot on the stove top. On copper vessels, the tin lining may pull away, and other pots will get burned bottoms before you realize it.

Teakettles

The teakettle was the first utensil that had its own special space on the wood stove top and it has rarely left. Moisture from the teakettle counteracted the dry wood heat and kept furniture from cracking. The teakettle could be made of many metals in many styles to give a woman a chance to express her personality.

When you put your teakettle on your wood stove to provide room moisture, you unknowingly started your new cooking career. The teakettle is one of the most important wood stove utensils. In addition to standing ready with a cup of tea, it can replenish moisture lost in cooking pots and hold hot water for gelatin and sauces. And if unexpected guests drop by, you can add water to the soup and have enough to go around—one of my grandmother's old tricks.

Stand an attractive jug of water by the stove to add to the teakettle as needed. To remove mineral deposits that build up in the kettle, rinse it with white vinegar. Or keep an oyster shell inside to avoid flaky water. So you will not burn out the bottom, put marbles in the kettle. If the kettle goes dry, the marbles will pop around and alert you.

(An aromatic way to keep moisture in the air is to put a small pan of water on the stove with cinnamon and cloves floating in it. A tasty way is to put apples, cored and filled with cinnamon and sugar, in this water pan. Your children will enjoy this afternoon snack as did the children of yesteryear.)

Stockpots

You will need a large pot with a heavy bottom and two handles to use as a stockpot. Cooks of old bemoan the loss of the stockpot that sat over low heat at the back of the stove to collect water drained from vegetables, scraps of meat, vegetable trimmings, fish heads, and any other would-be discards. After a few days, they strained the stock, flavored it with herbs and spices, and added new vegetables for one of the tastiest soups you can imagine.

Lids

Use lids on pots when you want to keep moisture in cooking meats and vegetables. For foods that you want to simmer into paste form or dehydrate, such as stocks, tomato sauces, applesauce, or apple butter, cook without a lid. Cook vegetables that grow under the ground with a lid and those that grow above the ground without one. Lids reduce cooking time in any case and are a necessary aid when steaming foods.

Trivets

Collect an assortment of trivets to put under cooking vessels. Because a wood stove has no buttons to push or knobs to turn to raise or lower cooking temperatures, you do it by raising or lowering the pots. When baking with a baking pan that sits directly on the stove top, use a trivet under it to prevent burning on the bottom.

Cast-iron trivets work well (but be sure to remove any rubber or plastic feet before putting them on the stove top). They were a special delight to old wood stove cooks, who chose them in round or triangular shapes with designs of stars and hearts, eagles and Victorian flourishes—"Purity, Truth, Love," they read. But you may use canning jar lids, small cans with both lids removed, or a door spring coiled up.

Accessories

Griddles are one of the earliest and most effective of cooking utensils. The designs of the past have continued to be useful today. The cast-iron griddles are sold in standard sizes. The soapstone griddle used in early New England kitchens is available in native Vermont stone and can be bought to put atop the stove. Nonstick by nature, it absorbs wood heat quickly yet readily gives up flapjacks and eggs when they are done. Scour it with salt to keep it smooth, and let it cool on the stove to avoid cracking from sharp temperature changes.

Small ovens for the wood stove also are available. Flue ovens of dual wall construction fit onto the stovepipe for holding small baking pans and for warming and drying foods. Camp stove ovens that are gathering dust in your garage can be used on the stove. One company manufactures a stove top oven specifically for a domestic air limited stove. But you can bake successfully on any stove top by inverting a roasting pan over a baking pan set on a trivet.

The Fire

A good fire made with proper wood is as basic to successful cooking as the food ingredients. Each wood has its own distinctive characteristics for cooking. Fruitwoods, for example, have excellent coaling qualities, and can be used for broiling. For more information about wood, see "Ten Wood Tips" and "Heat Value of Woods."

All wood should be dry and seasoned. To check, split off a kindling-sized piece of wood. If it snaps easily over your knee it is dry enough. Cut logs about eighteen inches long, or a convenient size for your firebox.

Mrs. E. E. Kellog advises in her cookbook of the 1800s that three logs burned at a time are better than one or two. Add fuel before the fire burns too low and keep a constant fire.

She also says it is a "common mistake to suppose that the draft of a stove must be kept open to gain greater heat. Only just enough air should be supplied to promote combustion. Fuel is wasted with too much draft." The more air you allow in the firebox, the more fuel you burn, but you do not necessarily get more heat.

Regulate drafts on the stove itself and on the stovepipe if necessary. Adjust thermostats on airtight stoves. Or open drafts—enough to let the air flow—in the top and bottom of other air limited stoves.

Start the Fire. Adjust the draft. Feed the fire constantly.

Temperature

Within thirty to sixty minutes after you light the fire, your stove will be ready for cooking. Stove top temperatures can range from 150 to 700 degrees Fahrenheit. Adjust the stove drafts for a steady heat. The wood you burn and the size of the logs determine the stove top temperature for cooking. Split a pile of quick burning wood to keep on hand to rev up the fire for quick cooking and raise the top surface temperature quickly. In stoves with baffle systems, more hot air is forced to the front of the stove, and the hot spot is close to the front of the unit. On other stoves it may be the spot directly above the center of the fire. When you need the highest heat for cooking, put the pot or pan here. Locate the cooler spots for simmering, melting, and other low-heat needs. Old-time cooks still moan the loss of the traditional "back-of-the-stove" where so many culinary needs were met. We have it back again—although on the new model wood heat stoves it may be the side or front of the stove where you find this subtle heat.

Judge the stove top temperatures for cooking with one of the methods used by wood stove cooks for many years—listen to the sound of the teakettle. When it hisses and gurgles, the water is boiling and you can quick cook or sauté. When steam rises gently and quietly from the spout, you can simmer or poach. Learn the language of your own teakettle.

Grandma spit on her finger and tapped the stove surface. When she heard the sizzle she started cooking. Spew a few drops of water on the surface and wait for the sizzle. You can melt butter in a saucepan and cook when it is hot enough to sauté an onion. Or you can be less adventuresome and use a stove thermometer that attaches magnetically to the surface to know exactly when to start.

Methods

Most of the following methods will work on all stoves. Some require removable burner lids and so will not apply to every stove. Now that you know your stove's possibilities, have collected your utensils, started the fire, and judged cooking temperature, you are ready to adapt cooking methods to the wood stove.

You can cook on, around, and in your stove. You can bake or cook in the ashes, and cook slowly with casseroling, simmering, poaching, and steaming. Or you can cook quick foods, broil, stir-fry, and also bake. Here's how.

Ash Cookery

Tough-skinned vegetables such as potatoes, acorn squash, and corn cook nicely in the firebox ashes, as do fish, cornmeal ash cakes, and stuffed apples. The American Indians were experts in ash cookery and taught settlers to cook squash this way.

To cook in the ashes, allow a bed of ashes to build up for three to five days, then cook in them just before stove-cleaning time. Collect ashes in a pile inside the firebox away from burning logs and fiery coals. Wrap the food in foil, or put it in unwrapped. Tuck the food into the ashes. Or put it in a cast-iron pot with a tight lid. Pull ashes around the sides of the pot. Check the food occasionally and remove it with tongs when it is done.

To cook potatoes, cover them with ashes when you let the fire die down at night, and eat them in the morning, or put them in when the fire is burning hot. (Be sure to watch them since potatoes sometimes explode.) If you object to ashes, wrap potatoes in foil. They steam rather than bake in this case, but you can enjoy the vitamin-rich skins. (You also can bake your potatoes on a rack inside a Dutch oven. Put potatoes in, cover, and cook on the stove top.) It will take thirty minutes to several hours for the potatoes to bake, depending on when you put them in and how hot the fire is burning. Remove them from the ashes with tongs. Then drop the hot potatoes into a pan of water and lift them out to dry in their own heat.

To cook corn on the cob in ashes, use fall varieties of corn on early fall fires. Soak unshucked corn in water for several hours, then shake off the water. Tuck the corn into ashes away from red-hot coals and leave it about ten minutes. Remove it, shake off the ashes, take off the husks, and butter it.

You also can cook fish—whatever kind you have—in the ashes. Rub salt and lemon over a cleaned fish. Lightly stuff it (combine two tablespoons parsley, three dried and crushed leaves of tarragon, chopped green onion, salt, and pepper). Wrap several bacon pieces around the fish body, then tightly seal it in foil. Bury it in the ashes and bake until it is done, about seven minutes per inch of thickness. Check after twenty minutes.

For stuffed apples, remove cores and stuff the fruit with cinnamon, sugar, butter, nuts, and raisins. Wrap the apples in foil and put them in the ash bed to cook until they are soft and the filling is blended.

Surface and Sideline Cooking

Use the wood stove's special qualities for cooking. It is an overall hot surface area for cooking, with dry and gentle heat on the back and edges. Use the stove top surface as a griddle, toaster, warmer, dryer, or buffet. Or put a griddle—soapstone, cast iron, or aluminum—directly on the stove top, or remove burner lids and connecting pieces on cast-iron stoves, to cook quick foods. Use the back of the stove to dry croutons or bread crumbs, warm breads, or melt butter and fondues. Anything that requires a melting temperature—butter for baking, cheese sauces—works well on the "back-of-the-stove."

Cook English muffins, quick ethnic breads such as chapati, tortillas, or lefse (see "Breads" in Index) directly on the stove top. Toast bread right on the surface hot spot. To warm breads and rolls, slice, butter, and wrap them in foil, and place on the back of the stove or other low heat area.

To make croutons for salads or soups, place leftover bread, cut in

cubes, on a cookie sheet. Let it sit on the back of the stove or other low heat area, stirring occasionally, until the bread is dried. Before using, melt butter or heat olive oil in a large saucepan. Add a garlic clove and/or paprika, salt, and pepper. Toss the croutons in the mixture.

To make fine bread crumbs for coatings, stuffings, and croquettes, save odds and ends of leftover bread and crackers. Dry them on cookie sheets set on a trivet on the back of the stove. When they are dry, roll them on a board with a rolling pin. Old World cookery traditionally uses bread crumbs in melted butter for coating dumplings, vegetables, or anything else that needs a final touch before serving.

Casseroling

The French form of casseroling—cooking in a pot with a tight-fitting cover over low heat—is ideal for the wood stove top. The slow cooking is especially good for tough cuts of meat as continual self-basting tenderizes the meat.

Layer raw vegetables and meat, together or separately, in a greased casserole dish that has a tight-fitting lid. Add a small amount of liquid that will condense with juices of the meat or vegetables. (Reduce liquid to one-fourth when adapting an American recipe that requires cooking a casserole *uncovered* in a conventional oven.) Cover the casserole and place it on a trivet on the low heat part of the stove. Simmer until the ingredients are tender and the liquid has turned into a sauce.

Simmering

Tough meats and vegetables meet their match with a wood stove. Recipes for slow cookers, which use heat in the 150 to 180-degree range, adapt ideally to the wood stove. Long, slow simmering tenderizes tough meat cuts and even old Tom turkeys and stewing hens. (Choose round, rump, chuck, flank, brisket, short ribs, shoulder, shank, and neck for economy cuts.)

For years, southerners have simmered their greens on wood stove tops. They use the juice of vegetable greens cooked with a scrap of pork for dipping corn bread and call it "pot likker." The highly nutritious greens, corn bread, and liquid can be a whole meal for a true "Rebel."

Stocks simmered on the stove add further economy to your wood stove cookery. Scraps of meat and vegetables become what the French call *fonds de cuisine* because they are the foundations of cooking that make soups and sauces have extra flavor. (See "Soups" in Index for basic stock recipes.) Use a pot with a heavy gauge metal bottom and two lifting handles.

Soups simmer on the stove and have more nutrients and flavor as a result. Stews make their own juices and are halfway between a soup and a plate dish when they are done.

To simmer meat, put it in a large kettle and add enough water—about an inch—to keep it from sticking to the pan and to tenderize it. Add herbs, seasonings, and vegetables as you wish. Cover and simmer it for several hours on the low heat part of the stove, using a trivet if the food seems to be sticking to the bottom of the pan. Tie up the legs of small turkeys and chickens to keep them handsome after their bout in the pot. To cook vegetables, place them in a pot, add liquid, and cook as you did the meat.

Dried beans of all varieties simmer nicely in their first cooking on the long, low wood fires. Cover beans with fresh water after soaking them for several hours or overnight. *Never add salt, sugar, tomatoes, or lemon to beans before this first cooking or they will not soften up properly.* Add one-eighth teaspoon soda if you live in a hard-water area. Cook beans until tender and drain. You lose very little iron, calcium, and potassium if you drain off the cooking water, and you improve the digestibility of the beans by doing so. Use the cooked beans in a chosen recipe. (Lentils and split peas can be used in recipes without precooking.)

Cooking of fruit and vegetable sauces that requires long cooking times to reduce moisture is perfect for the wood stove top. Try apple butter, tomato sauce, sauerkraut, catsup, or plum sauce. Mix up the concoction in the kitchen and put it on the low heat part of the stove to simmer until thick.

Poaching

While simmering is a "liquid that grins," poaching is a "liquid that barely smiles." The gently shivering water leaves delicate foods intact after cooking. Eggs, fish, and dumplings shiver to perfection in a pan of water over wood heat.

Poach an egg by putting a few drops of vinegar and salt to taste in water that is simmering in a wide pan. Break the egg into the center of the water and gently lift water over the egg until it is ready to eat.

To poach fish, open a flexible steamer rack in a saucepan and add enough water to cover the fish. Add herbs and seasonings to the water, then lower the fish into the liquid and let it poach seven minutes per inch of thickness of the fish. Lift the fish out of the steamer on the rack. (You also can place the fish on cheesecloth and lower it into a saucepan.)

Dumplings were developed by peasants in Europe as a way to turn tidbits of food into something special. Poach them as you would in conventional stove top cooking. Leave the pot uncovered until the dumplings rise to the top. Then cover. Tilt the lid a little to let excess steam escape.

Steaming

Steaming is a relic of open hearth days when the complete dinner was layered in one pot and puddings and breads were set in a bath of steam to cook until they were moist and tender. It is one of the most economical means of cooking because it needs only enough heat to turn a small amount of water into steam, which does the cooking.

Even today New Englanders and southerners cherish one-pot meals of meat and vegetables layered together and steamed through. For vegetables and small pieces of meat, place the steamer rack in a large saucepan holding enough water to cover the bottom. Put the pan on the hot spot of the stove top and steam until the texture and color tell you the food is done.

Or place a large cut of meat or a fowl in a small amount of liquid in a large pot, season, and cover tightly. Put the pot on the stove and cook for the majority of the allotted cooking time. Then layer vegetables over the meat and cook until tender. Serve vegetables and meat separately on the same platter.

Steaming sets puddings and softens grains in heavy breads. Fill a mold or can two-thirds full with pudding or bread dough. Place on a rack inside a large kettle that has a lid and add one or two inches of water to the kettle. Put it on the stove and bring the water to a simmer. Place the mold or can, covered tightly with foil tied with string, on the rack. Cover the kettle with its lid. Steam on the stove top two to three hours until a broom straw or knife comes out clean.

Baking

Ovens are a "modern" invention that have made baking so convenient they have become taken for granted in America just in the past fifty years. The first ovens in wood cookstoves were not ventilated so the flavor and aroma of the baked goods stayed in the food. That is one good reason why things never taste like "Grandmother used to make"—until now! When we go back and bake on the wood stove top, we get the same results because we use inverted pan systems and trivets.

Place the chosen baking pan on a trivet on the stove top, then cover it with a larger pan that allows two inches of space on the sides and four inches above. (A roasting pan will cover two cake pans.) You will find pans in your kitchen that match up to get the right baking combinations. This works for cakes, quick breads, and yeast breads, but do not expect your baked goods to brown. And do not try to cook finicky baked goods such as meringues and angel cakes that require a constant temperature.

To bake biscuits, scones, and other small items, dip them in melted butter and place them on a heated skillet or flat griddle. Cook them on one side, then flip them to finish cooking on the other side.

Use a Dutch oven to bake cakes, breads, and potatoes. For cakes and breads, put the Dutch oven on a trivet on the stove top and let it heat up. Then grease it, pour in the batter, cover it, and bake until a broom straw comes out clean. For biscuits or scones, place them in the Dutch oven, cover, and cook. Flip them once, gently, if you wish to brown both sides. Potatoes are just placed in the Dutch oven, covered, and baked.

Small ovens for the wood stove are available. Flue ovens of dual wall construction that fit onto the stovepipe hold small baking pans for warming and drying foods. Camp stove ovens gathering dust in your garage can be used on the stove. One stove company manufactures a stove top oven specifically for a domestic air limited stove (see "Mail Order Guide").

Quick Cooking

Sauté, stir-fry, pan fry, and cook any other foods that require a high temperature when the weather outside is cold and you need a roaring fire inside. This is the closest that wood stove cooking will come to your own electric or gas range cooking. But wood still has a gentle touch with the finished product. You can cook omelets, eggs, and pastas or stir-fry in a wok or pan fry chicken. When you use oil, test it for hotness with a few drips of water. Otherwise the food may be too greasy. Avoid fast frying unless you have a stove temperature of at least 350 degrees Fahrenheit. It is best to avoid deep fat frying because it is messy, the hot oil is dangerous, and it is hard to maintain a steady, even high temperature when you need to.

Locate the hot spot and put your utensil on it. To get a high heat, rev up the fire with small pieces of wood. If you have a removable pot hole lid, place the skillet or wok directly over the fire. Have the food at room temperature and use a lightweight skillet. Melt butter or heat oil and add the food to cook.

Stir-fry cooking in a wok came to us from Oriental Americans and has been picked up by the rest of us because it uses a small amount of meat and oil and cooks foods only long enough to heat them through and bring out flavor without losing nutrients. Heat oil in the wok. Chop bits of meat and vegetables. Stir them through the heated oil until they glisten, are warmed, and the meat is done.

To pan fry chicken, chops, or fish, heat a small amount of oil in a skillet. Add the chicken, chops, or fish that have been dipped in seasoned flour. Brown them on one side, then turn them over. Cover the pan and move it to a low heat part of the stove to cook for forty-five minutes or more until the meat or fish is done through.

To sauté onions, mushrooms, or pieces of meat, have the food at room temperature. To heat the butter or oil so the food literally "jumps" around the pan, use a skillet of a thin metal that evenly and steadily transmits heat.

Cook pasta, oatmeal, or anything else you want to try in a hurry when the stove is good and hot.

Broiling

Broiling is the process of exposing meat to open coals, which seals the surface of meat and causes the other fibers to hold in juices. This method can be used only with stoves that have removable pot hole lids or ones that have a door that lets you work comfortably inside the firebox over the coals.

Burn wood with good coaling qualities, such as fruitwoods (see "Heat Value of Woods"). When you are ready to broil, remove the burner lid from the stove top and place a cast-iron grill or wire rack over the hole. You may also open the stove doors and put an iron grill or rack, supported with rocks or bricks, inside the firebox. (If your stove smokes badly with the door open, you may want to avoid this method.) Place the meat to be cooked on the grill or rack. If you are cooking on the stove top, you may wish to place a large pot lid over the entire hole area. Cook meat on one side, then turn and cook on the other side. Steaks, hamburgers, fish, hot dogs, or chops take on a special flavor so satisfying you will not get impatient for spring and summer barbecue days.

Recipes

The "Eat America First" campaign of the early 1930s was led by Eleanor Roosevelt, wife of the thirty-second president of the United States, to encourage Americans to eat only American dishes, sans foreign flavor. But today we know that by eating the dishes of other countries we have been eating "America First" all along. Immigrants from around the world have come to our shores with recipes tucked in their apron pockets and created our unique American cuisine—a collage of ethnic foods.

This recipe collection reflects people and places, celebrations and wars, politics and movements that make the history of the United States. The recipes have come from people's recipe boxes across America, old cookbooks, historical archives, and magazines of preelectric days. Add your own family recipes to this collection and make history with new ones.

Criteria used in collecting the recipes will spare you boiled bear paws and possum meat. Each dish uses easy-to-get ingredients, is simple and mess-free to prepare, uses economy meats and vegetables, is tasty to the modern palate, can be cooked on all styles of stoves, and dates prior to the influx of gas and electric stoves into American homes.

Directions for cooking are not precise about minutes and degrees. You have to watch the food, instead of the clock, and know how "done" looks. But you will soon learn, whether you started your cooking career in the echo of wedding bells, in a bachelor pad, or in the kitchen at your mother's knee from the time you were old enough to stir the pudding.

Although the recipes are modernized, you will find yourself testing with a broom straw and pampering pots according to the kind of wood you burn, the style of your stove, the utensils you choose, and whether the weather outside is snowy or mild. You can cook any of the recipes on your modern range if you use a low, simmer burner or put a heat diffuser on the stove eye. For fine baking, we give conventional oven instructions to make this book a full value to you—on or off the wood stove.

Soups and Beverages

A cup or bowl of brew peps up palates and soothes social occasions around the wood stove. Dolley Payne Madison (1768–1849) knew this. For sixteen years as the dazzling and thoughtful hostess for President Thomas Jefferson and her husband, James, she greeted White House guests with a cup of bouillon as they came in from a snowy Washington night.

Stocks

Before cooks mastered the can opener, stockpots were the secret of good soups. As the catchall pot simmered long and slow on the back of the wood stove, the cook threw in fish heads, knucklebones, and vegetable bits to create flavorful and nutritious bases for soups, as well as sauces and casseroles.

Stocks can be distinct in flavor—chicken, beef, fish, or vegetable. Or they can be the hodgepodge flavor of would-be scraps and trimmings. Clarified with egg white and strained through cheesecloth, stock becomes bouillon or consommé.

Now that wood heat is back, you can retire your can opener, put a pot on the stove top, and revive the art of fine soup making.

Beef Stock

Beef trimmings*   6 pounds
Bay leaf   1
Large onion   1, chopped
Medium carrots   4 or 5, sliced
Parsley   5 sprigs, chopped
Leeks   1 or 2, sliced, white part only
Peppercorns   10
Celery   3 stalks, with leaves, sliced
Salt   2 tablespoons
Dry red wine   1 cup or
    Vinegar   1 to 2 tablespoons
Water   4 quarts

Place ingredients in stockpot. Add water and bring to simmer. When stock has simmered about 3 or 4 hours, remove from heat and cool. Strain through wet cheesecloth over a sieve, then refrigerate. Remove hardened fat from top. Makes about 3 quarts.

* Soup bones, scrap bones, and other beef bits.

Chicken Stock

Chicken scraps*   6 pounds
Medium onion   1, chopped
Medium carrots   3 or 4, sliced
Leeks   2, including green part, chopped
Celery   3 stalks, with leaves, sliced
Bay leaf   1
Peppercorns   6
Parsley   4 sprigs, chopped
Dry white wine   1 cup
Salt   2 tablespoons
Water   4 quarts

Place ingredients in stockpot and add water. Bring to simmer and cook uncovered 3 to 4 hours. Remove from heat and cool. Strain stock through wet cheesecloth over a sieve. Refrigerate, then skim off fat. Use immediately, refrigerate, or freeze. Makes about 3 quarts.
* Bones, wings, necks, backs, and other scraps.
Variation: Add a whole chicken to the stock mixture during the last hour of cooking. Remove chicken and serve immediately or use later in chafing dish cookery, casseroles, or salads.

Fish Stock

Fish scraps*   1½ pounds
Medium onion   1, chopped
Celery   2 ribs, chopped
Medium carrot   1, sliced
Parsley   2 sprigs, chopped
Lemon   3 slices
Peppercorns   8
Salt   1 scant teaspoon
Dry white wine   ¾ cup
Water   3 cups

Combine all ingredients in stockpot and simmer uncovered several hours. Strain through wet cheesecloth over a sieve. Use for poaching fish or as a soup base. Makes about 1 pint.
* Tail, head, backbone, and so on.

Vegetable Stock

Butter ½ cup
Turnips 3, peeled and sliced
Carrots 3, peeled and sliced
Onions 3, peeled and sliced
Celery 1 bunch, sliced
Leeks 4, cut in pieces, white part only
Garlic clove 1, minced
Parsley 2 sprigs, chopped
Dried thyme ¼ teaspoon
Dried rosemary ¼ teaspoon
Dried marjoram ¼ teaspoon
Salt 1 teaspoon
Peppercorns 1 teaspoon
Grated nutmeg pinch
Wheat bran 3 cups
Water 3 quarts

Melt butter in stockpot. Stir in next 6 ingredients until vegetables are well coated with butter. Add next 8 ingredients and stir. Add water and simmer uncovered 3 hours or more. Strain stock through wet cheesecloth over a sieve. Use as base for soup or add croutons, pasta, or rice, and cook until tender, then serve. Makes about 2 quarts.

Bouillon

Beef Stock (see Index) 10 cups
Beef trimmings* 2 pounds
Medium carrot 1, sliced
Leek 1, sliced
Celery 1 stalk, with leaves, sliced

Place ingredients in stockpot. Slowly bring to a boil and simmer uncovered about 2 hours. Cool, then strain through several layers of wet cheesecloth over a sieve. Refrigerate. When cold, remove hardened fat from top. Use immediately, refrigerate, or freeze. Serves 8.
* Scrap bones, soup bones, and so on.

Consommé

Bouillon (see Index)   4 cups
Egg whites   2
Eggshell   1, crushed
Cognac or other spirits   (optional)

Beat egg whites with a fork. Put into bouillon and add eggshell. Put bouillon over heat and bring to boil, constantly beating with a whisk until egg whites rise to the surface. Strain through a sieve covered with cheesecloth. Let liquid slowly seep through without forcing it. Reheat, add cognac if desired, and use immediately, refrigerate, or freeze. Serves 4.

Lamb-Cabbage Soup

To ensure that early Americans relied on her for wool, Mother England hindered import of sheep to the New World. But that did not stop the colonists, for sheep were vital to them. They simply learned to smuggle the animals past the English authorities. Such sheep, bred with stock brought in by Spanish explorers in the 1500s, became a flourishing flock by the 1700s. Cooks then could dare to kill lambs (sheep under one year old) for such recipes as this.

Lamb shoulder   1 pound, trimmed and cut in 1-inch cubes
Butter   1 tablespoon
Oil   1 tablespoon
Onion   1, chopped
Water   2 quarts
Salt and pepper   to taste
Large potato   1, peeled and diced
Small cabbage   1, cut into wedges
Parsley   1 tablespoon chopped

Brown lamb in butter and oil in a soup pot. Add onion and sauté. Add water and seasonings and simmer about 1 to 2 hours until lamb is tender. Add potato and cabbage. Simmer about 30 to 60 minutes until done. Garnish with parsley. Serves 6.

Scotch Broth

Upper-class Scottish bachelors—the first of their countrymen to come to colonial cities—were prize catches for Puritan daughters. Next came lowland artisans and laborers indentured to Virginia tobacco colonies and New York industries. The last major wave of Scottish immigrants came after 1763 crop failures. Whole clans of Scottish Highlanders came to settle North Carolina's mountainous and Cape Fear regions. Scotch broth they brought with them was so economical and tasty it has stayed in our diet through the years.

Lamb neck or shoulder with bones   2 pounds, cut into 6 pieces
Water   2 quarts
Barley   2 tablespoons
Salt   2 teaspoons
Pepper   ⅛ teaspoon
Carrots   ½ cup finely chopped
Turnips   ½ cup finely chopped
Onion   ½ cup finely chopped
Leeks   ½ cup finely chopped
Celery   ½ cup finely chopped
Parsley   1 tablespoon finely chopped

Put lamb and water in 5-quart casserole. Simmer about 2 hours until meat boils off bones. Skim off foam from surface. Add barley, salt, and pepper. Simmer on back of stove at least 1 hour. Add next 5 ingredients and cook about another hour until vegetables are tender. Lift lamb from soup and pick meat from bones and gristle. Cut meat into cubes, then return meat to soup and heat through. Adjust seasonings to taste and garnish with parsley to serve. Serves 6.

Brunswick Stew

Politicians dressed in white suits can still be found stumping on podiums shaded by magnolia trees. For such festive occasions back in 1828, squirrel was first stewed up in Brunswick County, Virginia. (Brunswick County, Georgia, disagrees.) My grandmother quickly substituted chicken, beef, and other meats for the squirrel, even though she had an abundance of the pesky creatures that "Pop" controlled with his slingshot. Alas, he used squirrel tails on his hand-carved wooden rocking horses and fed squirrel meat to his dog John.

Chicken, beef, pork, or squirrel   3 to 4 pounds
Water   4 quarts
Celery   2 stalks, with leaves
Large onion   1, chopped
Bell pepper   1, diced (optional)
Tomatoes   4 cups chopped
Lima beans   2 cups
Carrots   4, peeled and diced
Large potatoes   3, peeled and cubed
Corn   3 cups
Butter or margarine   ¼ cup
Salt   to taste
Pepper   ½ teaspoon
Cornstarch or tapioca   1 tablespoon
Cayenne   dash
Worcestershire sauce   ½ teaspoon

Put meat and water in a heavy soup pot, and cook 2 or more hours until meat falls off bones. Cool, then remove meat from stock and cube meat. Add next 6 ingredients to stock. Put pot on trivet, cover pot, and cook about 3 hours, stirring occasionally to keep beans from sticking to bottom of pot. Add remaining ingredients, including meat. Simmer uncovered about 30 minutes until mixture is well blended. Serves 16.

Mandu

The 18-year-old son of a Korean Confucian scholar spent his last four dollars for a hotel room in New York city in 1921. Penniless, Younghill Kung went to an Oriental restaurant and composed a poem about vegetable soup as a way of introducing himself to the manager and wrangling credit for a meal a day. He went from houseboy to Harvard student and proved himself "one of the most brilliant minds of the east" to fellow writer Pearl S. Buck. His books, The Grass Roof, East Goes West, *and* The Happy Grove *are small examples of the many contributions that Korean immigrants have made to American culture in science, literature, religion, art, athletics, and business since 1902. This soup comes from a Korean-American descendant, also a determined writer.*

Hamburger ½ pound, lean
Pork ½ pound, ground
Ginger ½ teaspoon freshly grated
Garlic 1 clove, minced
Spring onions 1 bunch, bulb and tops, chopped
Won ton wrappers ½ pound
Chicken Stock (see Index) 2 quarts
Soy sauce 1 teaspoon

In a bowl, mix hamburger, pork, ginger, garlic, and onions. Place ½ teaspoon of mixture in each won ton wrapper. Fold 3 corners into center. Wet last corner and seal over all. Pour stock and soy sauce into a deep kettle and place on stove top. When hot, add won tons and cook 20 to 30 minutes. Remove won tons from kettle with slotted spoon and serve separately with broth. Serves 6.

Puerto Rican Soup

The island of Puerto Rico is the only known spot where Christopher Columbus actually put his foot on United States soil. Today the island is a self-governing commonwealth under United States protection. Citizens move unhampered by immigration laws from island to mainland. Many were attracted to New York City's cigar and garment industries. They brought us this soup made satisfying with produce like they knew from their own fertile farmlands.

Ham ½ cup diced
Shortening 4 tablespoons
Onions 1 cup chopped
Green peppers 1 cup chopped
Medium tomatoes 3, peeled and chopped
Garlic cloves 2, minced
Tomato sauce ½ cup
Chicken Stock (see Index) 2 quarts
Rice 1 cup uncooked
Salt 1½ tablespoons
Shrimp 2 pounds
Peas 1 pound
Olives ½ cup pitted and chopped
Pimientos ¼ cup chopped

Sauté ham in shortening until lightly browned. Add next 4 ingredients, then stir and cook until vegetables are tender. Stir in next 4 ingredients and simmer about 30 to 60 minutes until rice is done. Add shrimp and peas and cook about 15 minutes until done. Stir in olives and pimientos and serve hot from the stove top. Serves 6.

Cioppino

Immigrant Italian fishermen take credit for this fish dish (pronounced "cho-peen-o"), which originated in the early 1900s on Fisherman's Wharf in San Francisco. Made with the catch of the day—whatever that might be—it is seldom cooked the same anywhere. Use your favorite local fish and serve this dish with Italian bread and California red wine—and napkins!

Firm saltwater fish   3 pounds
Dungeness crab   1
Large shrimp   1 pound uncooked
Clams, oysters, and mussels   12 total, unshucked
Large onions   2, chopped
Large green pepper   1, chopped
Olive oil   ¼ cup
Tomatoes   28-ounce can
Tomato juice   16-ounce can
Salt   1 to 2 teaspoons
Dried basil   ½ teaspoon
Pepper   ⅛ teaspoon
Garlic cloves   2, minced
Bay leaf   1
Dry red wine   2 cups
Parsley   1 tablespoon chopped

Cut fish into serving pieces. Crack crab and remove meat. Peel and devein shrimp. Steam clams, oysters, and mussels, then remove top shells of clams and reserve liquid. Remove and discard shells of oysters and mussels. Place fish and crab in 8-quart Dutch oven, reserving shrimp and clams. In skillet, sauté onions and green pepper in oil. Stir in clam liquid, tomatoes, tomato juice, and seasonings. Simmer uncovered 15 minutes, then stir in wine. Pour this mixture over fish and crab, heat until mixture simmers, then continue to simmer another 30 minutes. Add shrimp and simmer about 10 more minutes. Arrange clams on half shell on top and simmer another few minutes until they are heated through. Garnish with parsley and serve. Serves 10 to 12.

Seafood Gumbo

In southern Louisiana, "gumbo" means a mixture—maybe a dialect spoken by descendants of African slaves mixing French with their native tongue; maybe a soup that combines the profusion of seafood from the region's coastal waters; maybe Louisiana itself, a blend of many peoples, cultures, and customs. Fish of either the East or West coast makes this "mixture" just as tasty.

Bacon   6 strips
Butter   2 tablespoons
Flour   6 tablespoons
Green onions   2 bunches, chopped
Large onion   1, chopped
Parsley   ½ cup chopped
Bell pepper   1, chopped
Tomatoes   2, peeled and chopped
Hot water   3 quarts
Salt   to taste
Medium shrimp   1 pound, peeled and deveined
Crab meat   2 cups
Oysters   2 cups
Filé powder*   2 tablespoons
Rice
Hot pepper sauce   garnish

Cook bacon in skillet. Drain and save 2 tablespoons drippings. Add butter to drippings, gradually add flour, and make dark brown roux by stirring constantly to brown flour. Do not scorch it. This vital step may take up to 15 minutes. Add onions (reserving 1 cup green onion tops for garnish), parsley, and bell pepper. Cook, stirring constantly, about 10 minutes. Put this mixture, tomatoes, water, and salt in large pot. When soup begins to simmer, add shrimp and crab. Cook about 20 minutes. Add oysters and cook 10 more minutes. Stir a few tablespoons of the hot liquid into the filé powder and return to pot, stirring well. Garnish with green onions and serve with rice and hot pepper sauce. Serves 6 to 8.
* Finely ground young leaves of sassafras tree used to thicken soups and stews. Your local fish market may be willing to order it specially for you or to have it on hand.

Oyster Stew

"Oyster mania" flourished in the 1800s when people craved an oyster-a-day for health and happiness. Street peddlers hawked the high-protein shellfish and oyster bars were a daily stop for city dwellers. Express trains from Baltimore delivered the delicacies across the Alleghenies to oyster eaters in distant towns faster than they could receive their mail. Oysters, harvested from some three thousand twisted miles of Chesapeake Bay shoreline by Maryland watermen in small sailboats called skipjacks, have been cooked this way by generations of Marylanders.

Oysters   1 pint shucked, reserving liquor
Half-and-half   1 quart
Salt and pepper   to taste
Butter or margarine   ¼ cup cut in slices
Paprika   garnish

In a 2-quart saucepan, heat oysters with liquor until it comes to a boil and oysters are hot. Slowly add half-and-half, salt, and pepper, and heat through but do not boil. Spoon 5 to 6 oysters into each bowl. Top with butter. Pour hot milk over all and sprinkle with paprika. Serves 4 to 6.

Bean Soup

"Oregon fever" raged through the Mississippi Valley in 1842. Afflicted Americans piled their possessions into canvas-covered wagons and walked across plains and mountains—leaving a friend or relative buried in their wagon ruts every mile of the way. Those who survived the Oregon Trail dined on "beans, bacon and biscuits and biscuits, bacon and beans," according to one diarist. Some experts recommended that emigrants carry sixty pounds of beans per person—way too much, but a clue to their importance. This soup has been glorified so even the diarist would enjoy it.

Navy beans 1 pound
Water
Large onion 1, chopped
Green pepper 1, chopped
Tomatoes 16-ounce can
Brown sugar 1 teaspoon
Worcestershire sauce 1 teaspoon
Mustard 1 teaspoon
Tabasco sauce ½ teaspoon
Ham bone or knuckle

Soak beans in water overnight and cook several hours until tender. Drain beans and cover with fresh water. Add remaining ingredients and cook several hours. Serves 6.

Baked Bean Soup

"Waste not, want not" was the rule of thumb for the Boston Puritans. On Monday they made soup out of Sunday's leftover baked beans.

Small onion ½, chopped
Butter 2 tablespoons
Leftover Boston Baked Beans (see Index) 2 cups
Water or Chicken Stock (see Index) 4 cups
Celery 1 stalk, chopped
Fresh tomatoes 3, peeled, seeded, and chopped or
　　Canned tomatoes 1 cup drained and chopped
Salt and pepper to taste

Sauté onion in butter in soup pot. Add remaining ingredients and simmer about 2 hours. Smash some of the beans with the back of a large spoon. Serves 4.

Depression Stew

While men sold apples on street corners and President Herbert Hoover anguished over surviving the Great Depression of the 1930s, women fed their families beans and cornmeal, if they were lucky. With the stock market crash, some twelve million Americans were out of work, banks failed, and businesses went bankrupt. Women turned to soybeans, which had been grown in the United States since 1804 chiefly as livestock feed, and made them into tasty dishes such as this stew. Serve it with corn bread to complete protein in soybeans.

Soybeans 1½ cups
Water
Medium tomatoes 6, peeled and chopped or
    Tomatoes two 16-ounce cans
Green pepper ¼ cup minced
Celery ¼ cup minced
Brown sugar 2 tablespoons
Lemon juice 1 tablespoon
Salt to taste
Fresh basil 1 leaf or
    Dried basil ¼ teaspoon
Potato 1, diced
Carrots 2, sliced diagonally
Pork sausage ½ pound, fried (optional)

Soak soybeans in water overnight. Cook in fresh water several hours or overnight, until tender. Drain and cover with water again, add next 7 ingredients, and cook about 30 minutes until ingredients are well blended. Add potato and carrots. Cook another hour on low heat part of stove. Add sausage, if desired. Serves 6 to 8.

German Lentil Soup

Southern states shipped cotton and tobacco to Germany in the 1800s. For the return trip to America, traders filled their ships with passengers—natives of Germany's Rhineland. While waiting on the docks for winds to sail and on the long sea voyage, the Germans played their trombones and sang anthems to keep their spirits up. Once in the New World, they continued to play and sing and were the first to popularize symphonic music. Their "Germania Orchester" of twenty-three members became the New York Philharmonic Orchestra. At singing society gatherings and songfests, a pot of this hearty lentil soup fared well, as it does today at a home sing or before the symphony.

Water
Smoked ham hock 1 or
    Soup bones several
Lentils 2 cups
Beef Stock (see Index) 2 cups
Medium carrot 1, chopped
Potatoes 1 cup diced
Medium onion 1, chopped
Celery ½ cup, with leaves, chopped
Vinegar 2 tablespoons
Salt to taste
Pepper to taste
Tomato paste 2 tablespoons
Parsley 2 tablespoons chopped
Tabasco sauce dash
German sausage 1½ cups sliced (optional)

Cover ham hock with water in soup pot and simmer several hours. Remove from pot, take meat off, and return to broth. Add remaining ingredients except sausage and simmer 2 hours. Smash lentils with back of a spoon, and add sausage if desired. Simmer another 30 minutes. Serves 6.

Swedish Pea Soup

On the banks of the Delaware River, fifty Swedes landed in 1638 to found New Sweden, but their venture has been lost in the pages of history. Their town of Fort Christina—now Wilmington, Delaware—was a group of log cottages, a chapel, and windmill. It later included a library and six hundred "people proper and strong of body...with fine children," one of whom became a signer of the Declaration of Independence. Their success with furs and tobacco threatened the Dutch who seventeen years later overtook them in a bloodless raid. Eventually the Swedes were Anglicized so all that remains of their venture are hints in architecture and Pennsylvania red cattle. Other Swedish immigrants have come into American society through the years, keeping alive our regard for their health-oriented lifestyle. This soup was easily transported to New World shores. Even today it is said to be served every Thursday at the Swedish king's table and throughout the land—with small sweet pancakes and hot punch.

Yellow peas   2 cups
Water
Cold water   6 cups
Fresh pork   1 pound
Salt   2 teaspoons
Ginger   ¼ teaspoon

Rinse and soak peas in water overnight. Drain, put in heavy soup pot with 6 cups cold water, then gently simmer 1 hour. Add pork and simmer 2 more hours. Season with salt and ginger. Remove pork from pan. Slice meat and serve it separately with soup. Serves 6.

Split Pea Soup

The Reverend Francis Higginson wrote home delightedly from America in 1629, "There is in Massachusetts a store of green peas as good as ever I ate in England now growing in the Governor's garden." The English ate pease porridge hot, cold, and nine days old. Moreover dried split peas have been insurance against hunger from the days of ancient Troy to the settling of America. No wonder peas moved west with so many ethnic groups—Scandinavians, Mormons, Irish—to thrive in the state of Idaho.

Dried split peas 2 cups
Water 2 quarts
Ham hock 1
Parsley 1 sprig, chopped
Bay leaf 1
Celery ½ cup, with leaves, finely chopped
Salt and pepper to taste
Water or milk for thinning

Place all ingredients in large soup kettle and simmer gently on low heat spot of stove top about 2 hours. Remove bay leaf and ham hock. Chop meat that comes off bone, then return ham bits to pea mixture and season with salt and pepper. If convenient, puree or sieve soup. Return to pot and heat, thinning to desired consistency. Serves 8 to 10.

Virginia Peanut Soup

Plantation masters and slaves alike rejected peanuts, except as pig feed, because they were the food thrown to Negroes in the horrid holds of African slave ships. Then some hungry Civil War soldiers chanced to roast them over their campfire and found them to be "excellent." Today such dishes as this peanut soup find their way into silver soup tureens in many fine southern restaurants, from historic Williamsburg, Virginia, to Plains, Georgia.

Butter ¼ cup
Celery 2 ribs, chopped
Medium onion 1, chopped
Flour 3 tablespoons
Chicken Stock (see Index) 2 quarts
Peanut butter 2 cups
Light cream 2 cups
Peanuts ¼ cup chopped (optional)

Put soup kettle on stove when hot and put in butter to melt. Add celery and onion and sauté. Stir in flour, then gradually add stock. Stir in peanut butter and mix well. Just before serving, stir in cream, and peanuts if desired, and heat through. Serves 6.

Corn Chowder

Europeans had never heard of corn until they ventured to America's shores. As they sampled native foods, they understood why the Indians worshipped the versatile grain. Some Europeans still disdain it as animal food, but Americans include it in their diets in many forms, as in this hearty chowder, originated by peasant fishermen of European stock.

Bacon 2 strips, diced
Onion ½ cup chopped
Celery ¼ cup chopped
Flour 2 tablespoons
Water 1 cup
Potatoes 1 cup diced
Salt ½ teaspoon
Pepper ⅛ teaspoon
Thyme ⅛ teaspoon
Frozen corn 10-ounce package
Milk 1½ cups
Pimiento 1, chopped
Light cream ½ cup
Parsley 1 tablespoon chopped

Cook bacon with onion and celery in heavy soup kettle. Add flour and cook another minute or so, stirring constantly. Add water, potatoes, and seasonings, and simmer about 10 minutes. Add corn and milk and simmer until vegetables are tender. Just before serving, stir in pimiento and cream and heat through but do not boil. Garnish with parsley. Serves 4.

Dutch Corn Soup

The Pennsylvania Dutch turned fertile limestone valleys of Pennsylvania into a giant vegetable garden, reminiscent of their native Rhineland. These native Germans earned reputations as superb cooks when they cooked up their produce into classic dishes for hungry Continental Congressmen in Philadelphia. This chicken and corn soup simmered for hours in large iron pots over open fires and served huge crowds.

Stewing chicken   4 pounds, cut up
Onion   1, chopped
Water   4 quarts
Carrot   1, sliced diagonally
Celery   ½ cup, with leaves, chopped
Salt   2 teaspoons
Pepper   to taste
Whole mixed pickling spices   1 teaspoon
Fresh corn   4 cups or
   Canned corn   1 quart or
   Frozen corn   three 10-ounce packages
Rivels
Eggs   2, hard cooked and chopped

In a large soup kettle, simmer chicken and onion in water about 1½ hours or until chicken is tender. Remove chicken from broth and strain stock. Cool chicken and stock, then skim fat from stock and cube chicken. Return chicken to stock, add next 6 ingredients, and simmer about 30 minutes. Add rivels and garnish with eggs. Serves 8.

Rivels

Flour   1 cup
Salt   ¼ teaspoon
Egg   1
Milk   1 teaspoon

Mix flour with salt. Stir in egg and milk until mixture crumbles like small peas. Drop these into soup. Cook 10 to 15 minutes.

Potato-Leek Chowder

Leeks became the national symbol of the Welsh after they won a historic battle with the vegetable stuck in their helmets to distinguish themselves from the enemy. This fine peasant soup cooks leeks appropriately on a wood stove. Historically, iron for stoves was made available because a Welsh immigrant, David Thomas (1794–1882) was "The Father of the American Iron Trade." His idea—that air forced into a blast furnace creates better iron—set off the industry that touches every phase of our lives—from paper clips and skyscrapers to wood stoves.

Small leeks   5, finely chopped or
    Large leeks   2, finely chopped
Butter   3 tablespoons
Flour   3 tablespoons
Chicken Stock (see Index)   2 cups
Medium potatoes   3, diced
Light cream   1½ cups
Salt   to taste
White pepper   to taste

Sauté leeks in butter in soup kettle, stir in flour, and cook about 10 minutes. Add stock and potatoes and simmer until potatoes are done. Add cream, salt, and pepper, and heat but *do not boil*. Serve hot or cold. Serves 4 to 6.
Variations: Add 2 cups precooked shrimp or ½ cup finely diced ham, or 1 cup chopped clams, and heat through just before serving.

Tomato Soup

Europeans called tomatoes "love apples" because they thought they were an aphrodisiac. They brought seeds to plant in their American flower gardens. Then, of all things, Thomas Jefferson dared to eat some. Today we take tomatoes for granted—on food, in food, and straight. Serve this soup on Valentine's Day, or whenever you feel loving.

Medium tomatoes   10
Medium onion   1, finely chopped
Butter   2 tablespoons
Flour   2 tablespoons
Hot Chicken Stock (see Index)   6 cups
Tomato paste   2 tablespoons
Cayenne   dash
Parsley   2 tablespoons finely chopped
Celery leaves   2 tablespoons finely chopped
Dried dill   1 teaspoon crushed
Salt   to taste
Pepper   to taste
Garlic croutons or taco chips   garnish

Briefly dip tomatoes in boiling water, then in cold water, then peel. Cut tomato in half, blossom end to stem end. Cup tomato in hand over a bowl and squeeze gently until most of the seeds are out, then chop tomatoes. In a soup kettle, sauté onion in butter, add flour, and stir. Stir in stock and simmer about 5 minutes, stirring constantly. Add tomatoes, tomato paste, and cayenne, and simmer 5 minutes. Add next 5 ingredients. Serve hot with croutons. Serves 6 to 8.

Potage Crécy   (Puree of Carrot Soup)

In the 1790s, French aristocrats found refuge from the French Revolution in Philadelphia, New York, Baltimore, and Charleston. Their manners and customs caught the fancy of Americans who, after their own revolution, were ready to reject everything English as well as gild the rough colonial life. (Inns and taverns became "hotels." Coffee houses became "cafés.") Even in the White House President Thomas Jefferson had a French cook, only to be chastened by the fiery Patrick Henry for "abjuring his native victuals." (Hundreds of Frenchmen who had never bothered to vote turned out in New York to support Jefferson in 1800.) After a day of elaborate meals, the typical Frenchman eats a bowl of soup with bread for supper. Potage Crécy is a fine soup for winter—made from an easy-to-store root vegetable.

Butter   2 tablespoons
Onion   ¾ cup finely chopped
Carrots   3 cups finely chopped
Chicken Stock (see Index)   1 quart
Tomato paste   2 teaspoons
Rice   2 tablespoons uncooked
Salt and white pepper   to taste
Heavy cream   ½ cup
Butter   1 tablespoon

Melt 2 tablespoons butter in a 4-quart saucepan on stove top. Stir in onions and cook until soft. Add next 4 ingredients and simmer until carrots are tender. Remove carrots and smash with back of a large spoon or return to kitchen and put in a blender. (Return soup to saucepan if you have blended it.) Season with salt and pepper, and stir in cream. Heat through but do not boil, then stir in 1 tablespoon butter. Serves 4.

Greens Soup

Pioneer women rejoiced at the green fields of fresh wild mustard that greeted them in California's Napa Valley at the end of a long journey on brown beans and bacon. Even today the wild greens are free for the picking there—between the rows of grape vines after the harvest.

Unsalted butter   1 tablespoon
Young mustard greens or kale   1 cup shredded
Chicken Stock (see Index)   2 cups
Egg yolks   4
Whipping cream   ½ cup
Zucchini   1 cup cut into strips
Fresh basil leaves   ¼ cup shredded
Pesto   3 tablespoons
Coarse salt   ½ teaspoon
Pepper   to taste

Melt butter in saucepan, then stir in greens and toss about 1 minute. Add stock and bring to boil, then let greens simmer until tender. In a small bowl, beat egg yolks with cream and stir in a small amount of hot soup. Return all to soup pot. Add remaining ingredients and stir until soup is thick enough to coat a wooden spoon. Serves 4.

Pesto

Fresh basil leaves   2 cups
Garlic cloves   2
Olive oil   ¼ cup
Fresh Parmesan cheese   3 tablespoons grated
Pine nuts   2 tablespoons toasted

Combine basil and garlic in blender to chop. Gradually add oil, then Parmesan and nuts, and blend until almost smooth. Store in freezer or refrigerator until needed.

Mushroom Soup

Early San Franciscans blended the cooking of the east and west of the United States and lands afar to develop a cuisine lavish with oyster cocktail, and shrimp and mushroom dishes. Chinese cooks prepared the dishes in homes and restaurants to the desires of their employers—"You want twenty-dollar-a-month cooking or twenty-five-dollar-a-month cooking?" This San Francisco soup is a twenty-five-dollar delicacy.

Leeks   ⅓ cup sliced
Onion   ⅓ cup sliced
Celery   ⅓ cup sliced
Mushrooms   3 cups sliced or diced
Butter   3 tablespoons
Flour   3 tablespoons
Chicken Stock (see Index)   3 cups
White wine   ½ cup
Thyme   ⅛ teaspoon
Salt and pepper   to taste
Light cream   1 cup

In a soup pot, sauté first 4 ingredients in butter, then stir in flour. Add remaining ingredients except cream and simmer 30 minutes. Stir in cream just before serving. Serves 6.

Vegetable Soup

As Anthony McAllister sailed on the Star of Persia *in 1871, he recorded this soup recipe in his personal log of 6 July. Not at all exotic, it uses non-perishable ingredients that would keep in the ship's hold and could be secured in most ports. While the soup is tasty enough, a love poem found on the following pages of his log speaks of his yearning for the one whose "promise churned my heart." His thoughts may well have been of her home-cooked meals.*

Carrots   2, scraped and diced
Onion   1, peeled and diced
Cabbage   ¼ pound, thinly sliced
Turnips   2, peeled and diced
Potatoes   2 medium, peeled and diced
Butter   2 tablespoons
Water   2 quarts
Lean beef   ½ pound, cut into ¼-inch pieces

Put carrots, onion, cabbage, turnips, potatoes, butter, and water into 8-quart soup kettle. Cook about 30 minutes. Add meat and cook another hour. Serves 6.

Fruit Soup

Earliest references to soup in the English language describe it as a sweet fruit concoction. This soup of that description was eaten at every hearty meal as a side dish or dessert by the Wyoming tie hacks. These men of Norwegian and Swedish heritage cut over ten million railroad crossties of lodgepole pine with brute strength, saws, and broad axes, and floated them out of the forests one hundred miles down the Wind River. Mechanization ended their era in the early 1940s, but "knights of the broadax" live on in a book of that title by Joan Trego Pinkerton. This fruit soup was their favorite dish.

Mixed dried fruit   1 pound
Raisins   1 cup
Water   2 quarts
Flour   2 tablespoons
Soda   ½ teaspoon
Cold water   ¼ cup

Cinnamon   1 teaspoon
Sweet or sour cream   2 cups
Butter   3 tablespoons
Sugar   ¼ cup or to taste
Sour or whipped cream   garnish

Put fruit in soup pot and cover with water. Simmer several hours or until tender. Make a paste of flour, soda, and cold water. Remove some liquid from fruit and stir in. Add paste to fruit, stir, then add cinnamon and cook 10 more minutes. Remove from heat, stir in 2 cups cream, then add butter and sugar. Reheat but *do not boil* and serve garnished with cream. Serves 6.

"Boiled" Coffee

An Englishman once ridiculed colonial Americans for drinking "syrup of soot, essence of old shoes." But the brew that kept people pushing down the Oregon Trail ("nothing but hardtack and coffee, and coffee and hardtack") today keeps Americans pushing through many varied activities. Served in almost every household, it has become our national drink. This is an economical way to enjoy it.

Drip grind coffee   2 tablespoons
Eggshell   from 1 egg
Cold water   ¼ cup
Boiling water   1 cup

Combine coffee, eggshell, and cold water in coffee pot or covered pot. Add boiling water and let simmer—not "boil"—for several minutes. Move to back of stove to keep hot, about 10 minutes. Just before serving, settle grounds with a small dash of cold water. Pour into cup, being careful not to disturb the grounds. Serves 1.

Chocolate Drink

Benjamin Franklin believed chocolate was a good medicine for any ailment. He brewed his chocolate on his new invention—a three-sided firebox that came out into his parlor. This ancestor of wood stoves gave off more heat than a fireplace, but also gave a view of the fire and a surface for cooking his daily potion.

Cocoa   2 teaspoons
Sugar   1 teaspoon
Water   ¼ cup
Milk   ¾ cup

Mix cocoa and sugar together in a small saucepan. Stir in water and simmer. Slowly add milk and heat through. Serves 1.

Mulled Cider

Teetotalers during the temperance movement of the 1830s axed away at whole apple orchards in their vengeance against the "Cider Age"—a time in American history when hard cider was more available than corn whiskey and everyone drank it for meals and refreshment. Heated and spiced, it tastes especially good on winter evenings.

Apple cider   2 quarts
Sugar   ½ cup or to taste
Cinnamon sticks   3
Whole cloves   6
Whole allspice   3
Orange   1, sliced
Raisins   1 tablespoon
Lemon juice   from ½ lemon

Combine all ingredients in a kettle and heat on back of stove. Stir to dissolve sugar. When heated through, serve right from the stove top. Serves 5 to 10.

Mulled Wine

For festive occasions, wood cooks of old heated everyday domestic wine and served it flavored with spices, as in this recipe. To heat the wine, they poured it into a "spider," a skillet with three legs to hold it up over hot coals, and stirred it with a "loggerhead," a long iron rod with a bulbous end.

Water 1 cup
Sugar or honey ½ cup
Orange zest of 1 orange or
    Lemon zest of 1 lemon
Whole cloves 10
Cinnamon stick one, 2 inches long
Burgundy wine 1-quart bottle
Freshly grated nutmeg garnish

Mix first 5 ingredients in kettle. Cover, heat, and simmer about 15 minutes. Stir in wine. When wine is heated through, strain into wine pot and ladle into mugs. Sprinkle with nutmeg. Serves 6 to 8.

Hot Buttered Rum

Rum caused the American Revolution as much as anything else. When the British Parliament passed the Molasses Act of 1733 to restrict our importation of molasses for making rum, it was one insult too many and they raised the ire of many colonists. Rum had been a long tradition and every navy recruit expected his daily ration of "grog."

Butter 1 tablespoon
Sugar 1 teaspoon
Boiling water ¼ cup
Dark rum ¼ cup
Freshly grated nutmeg garnish

Put butter in a warm tumbler and add sugar, boiling water, and rum. Top with nutmeg. Serves 1.

Side Dishes

Our wood-burning forebears cooked the foods they had on hand—unlike the bounty that fills our refrigerators from "fruited plains" many miles across our country. In history, these "side dishes" were main dishes, especially in winter months when dried beans, grains, and root crops filled the larders and wild game avoided the gun.

Rice Apples

Brother fought bitterly against brother in the Civil War (1861–1865) and cemented the United States of America into a nation from which no state could ever legally secede again. While war generals and politicians created new ideas—mines, telegraphy, photography, repeating rifles, the draft— an Iowa woman named Annie Wittenmeyer fretted over the diet of wounded soldiers. She created a booklet of recipes because "... hundreds of our brave soldiers have died of debility, who if sustained at the proper time with suitable food, might now be in the first ranks of the army..." One of her recipes is adapted here for peacetime palates.

Apples 6, cored
Rice 1 cup cooked
Seedless raisins ¼ cup
Almonds ¼ cup chopped
Brown sugar 1 cup
Water ½ cup
Ground cardamom ½ teaspoon

Peel top third (stem end) of each apple and place in buttered 9-inch square baking pan. Mix rice, raisins, and almonds together and fill apples. Mix sugar and water with cardamom and pour over apples. Tightly cover dish with foil or lid and place on trivet. Cook over low heat part of stove about 1 to 1½ hours until apples are tender. Serves 6.
Note: In a conventional oven, bake at 375° for 45 minutes.

58   Side Dishes

Risotto à la Milanèse

Thomas Jefferson, one of the founding fathers of our country, had a passion for growing food plants. Determined to raise the fine Italian strain of rice at his Monticello home in the Virginia hills, he smuggled a sampling of seed rice out of Italy in the late 1700s. He would have used this classic dish to prepare his yield.

Rice   2 cups uncooked
Turmeric   ¼ teaspoon
Butter   1 tablespoon
Beef or Chicken Stock (see Index)   4 cups
Butter   ½ cup
Parmesan cheese   1 cup grated

Put rice, turmeric, and 1 tablespoon butter into cold stock in a heavy saucepan with a tight-fitting lid. Stir and cook over low heat about 1 hour until rice has absorbed moisture. Stir in remaining butter and cheese until melted. Serves 6.

Pine Nut Pilaf

Shipping trade thrived at the Charleston, South Carolina, harbor, making it the richest city in the South before the Revolutionary War. Rice that filled the holes of ships leaving port and pine nuts that came in from foreign ports with Oriental rugs, spices, and slaves were combined in this South Carolina low country recipe.

Chicken Stock (see Index)   2 cups
Butter   2 tablespoons
Salt   ½ teaspoon
Rice   1 cup uncooked
Pine nuts   ½ cup
Chicken or shrimp   ½ cup cooked and chopped (optional)

Bring stock to boil in saucepan, then add salt and butter. Slowly add rice to boiling stock, cover, and cook over low heat part of stove for 30 minutes. Toss with nuts, and add chicken, if desired, just before serving. Serves 4 to 6.

Barley and Pine Nut Casserole

The Great Salt Lake region of Utah was the crossroads for many peoples—Indians, Brigham Young and his Mormon followers (1847), "resettled" Japanese after World War II, and waves of Greek, German, English, Spanish, and Italian settlers. All could create this regional dish from ingredients indigenous to the Salt Lake area.

Butter   6 tablespoons
Pine nuts   ⅓ cup
Barley   1 cup
Onion   1, chopped
Parsley   ½ cup minced
Green onions or chives   ¼ cup minced
Salt   ¼ teaspoon
Pepper   ¼ teaspoon
Beef or Chicken Stock (see Index)   3½ cups

Melt 2 tablespoons butter in saucepan. Sauté pine nuts until lightly browned. Add remaining butter, then sauté barley and onion. Remove pan from heat and stir in next 4 ingredients. Spoon into greased 1½-quart casserole and pour stock over all. Put on trivet on stove top, cover casserole, and cook about 1½ hours until liquid is absorbed and barley is tender. Serves 6.
Note: In a conventional oven, cook at 375° for 1 hour.

Chestnut Puree

Chestnuts were "chinquapins" to the Indians, who found them under native dwarf chestnut trees in the Appalachian Mountains. Today most chestnuts are imported because fungus wiped out the majority of the wild and domestic chestnuts around 1940. But the disease-resistant varieties that botanists planted after the blight are beginning to yield, and the sweet nuts are becoming more readily available. A chestnut puree is a delicious accompaniment to turkey or game.

Chestnuts 1 pound
Oil 1 teaspoon
Water
Vinegar 1 tablespoon
Celery 2 stalks, chopped
Small onion 1, chopped
Butter 2 tablespoons
Light cream 2 to 3 tablespoons
Salt to taste
Pepper ½ teaspoon

Gash flat side of each nut, put in pan with oil, and toss until coated. Cover pan and roast until skins fall off the nuts, or wrap them in foil and roast in ashes. Put nuts in saucepan, cover with water, and add vinegar, celery, and onion. Boil until tender, drain, and discard celery and onion. Puree chestnuts until they are free of lumps. Beat in butter, cream, salt, and pepper. Serves 4.

Apple-Stuffed Acorn Squash

American Indians ate squash centuries before they introduced it to the first white settlers. They roasted the squash whole before cutting into its hard outer shell, and filled the open cavity with sap from maple trees and a little bear fat (we use butter). When the settlers introduced the Indians to apples, the native Americans were so pleased with the fruit that they added it to their diet. They planted seeds in their villages and had their own trees in a few years.

Acorn squash 2
Tart apples 3, cored and diced
Raisins ¼ cup
Maple syrup ½ cup
Butter ¼ cup, melted
Butter 1 tablespoon

Place squash in steamer rack above simmering water and steam about 1 to 2 hours until almost tender. Remove, cut in half, and remove seeds. Place 4 halves cut side up on rack inside Dutch oven. Mix apples, raisins, syrup, and melted butter and put inside squash. Brush with remaining butter. Cover and put on trivet on stove top for about another hour until squash is soft and apples are tender. Serves 8.

Pompion Pye

Present day pies barely resemble the first pumpkin "pyes"—a whole pumpkin with the top cut off, seeds scooped out, milk poured in, then baked on an open hearth. This "receipt" for the "Great Round Pompion" was recorded by Englishman John Gerade in 1597 and is on file at Charles Towne Landing (1670), the restored historic site of the first permanent English settlement in South Carolina.

Pumpkin 1, small enough to fit into cast-iron pot
Tart baking apples 4 or enough to fill pumpkin, unpeeled, cored, and quartered
Raisins 1 cup
Honey ½ cup
Cinnamon 1 teaspoon
Water 1 cup

Cut off top (stem part) of pumpkin as if you were making a jack-o'-lantern, and clean out seeds. Mix next 4 ingredients together, then fill pumpkin to its full capacity. Replace the cut-off top of the pumpkin. Put pumpkin in cast-iron pot. Pour water in bottom of pot. Place on stove top and cook about 2 hours until pumpkin is soft. To serve, spoon out pumpkin with apples, raisins, and sauce. Serves 8.

Yams with Apples

Indians shared the wild yam (as well as squash) with the Pilgrims. This root vegetable could be stored for winter when there was little else to cook. It tasted good and was considered a relief for rheumatism.

Large yams   2, peeled
Tart apples   2, peeled, cored, and thinly sliced
Butter   2 tablespoons
Brown sugar   3 tablespoons
Nutmeg   ⅛ teaspoon

Slice yams ½-inch thick and boil in heavy pot, with lid on, until tender. Mix in apples, dot with butter, and sprinkle with sugar and nutmeg. Gently fold ingredients together. Tightly cover pot, place on trivet, and simmer on stove top about 1 hour until all ingredients are tender and blended. Serves 4.
Note: In a conventional oven, bake at 350° for 30 to 45 minutes.

Sweet Potato Casserole

Sweet potatoes were first grown in Virginia in the 1600s. As a root crop, they kept well through the winter and graced wealthy landowners' groaning boards—buffets so ladened with food that one always overate.

Sweet potatoes   3 pounds
Brown sugar   ¾ cup
Butter   ½ cup
Nutmeg   ½ teaspoon freshly grated
Light cream   about 2 cups
Sugar cubes   8, crushed

Cook potatoes in boiling salted water until tender. Drain, peel, and cut into ¼-inch slices. Layer slices in a buttered 3-quart casserole dish. Sprinkle layers with brown sugar and dot with butter. Sprinkle center layer with nutmeg. Pour in enough cream to cover potatoes. Sprinkle with nutmeg and sugar cubes. Set casserole on trivet on stove top and cover with lid. Let cook about 1½ hours until potatoes are covered with syrup. Serves 6 to 8.
Note: In a conventional oven, cook at 350° for 45 minutes.

Sweet Potato Pudding

Many black slaves owed their lives to the tasty sweet potato. Abundant with vitamins A and C and high energy value, sweet potatoes kept the farm worker alive and hoeing. With freedom and some prosperity, the black cook magically transformed the simple root into this rich pudding.

Sweet potatoes ½ pound, cut in pieces
Eggs 4, beaten
Butter ½ cup
Sugar 6 tablespoons
Nutmeg 1 teaspoon
Mace 1 teaspoon
Lemon juice of 1 lemon
Lemon peel of 1 lemon, grated
Sherry wine-glassful
Brandy wine-glassful

Simmer potatoes until tender, then peel and cream them. Add eggs, stirring gradually. Add remaining ingredients and put into buttered 9 by 13-inch baking dish. Cover and set on trivet on stove top. Cook about 1 hour until knife comes out clean. Serves 4.
Note: In a conventional oven, cook at 350° for 45 minutes.

Potatoes and Pineapple

Black scientist George Washington Carver (1864?–1942) experimented with the sweet potato and discovered that 118 different products, including starch, could be made from it. This elegant recipe from Iowa makes Carver's work hard to imagine.

Medium sweet potatoes 6, cooked
Pineapple slices 6, halved
Pineapple juice ¾ cup, drained from pineapple
Dark brown sugar ½ cup
Margarine ¼ cup
Butter ¼ cup
Butter flavoring ¼ teaspoon

Peel potatoes and slice in half lengthwise. Arrange alternating layers of sweet potatoes and pineapple in 9 by 13-inch baking pan. In saucepan on stove top heat together remaining ingredients. Let boil for 3 minutes. Put baking dish on trivet on stove top. Pour juice over potatoes and pineapple. Cover baking dish and cook about an hour until syrup thickens. Serves 4.
Note: In a conventional oven, bake at 350° for 30 minutes.

Hot German Potato Salad

Wherever there was sod to break and barren places to cultivate across our land, Germans were assets as settlers. This dish came with them to their homesteads on the unbroken prairies of South Dakota.

Medium potatoes   6, boiled in jackets
Bacon   6 strips
Onion   ¼ cup chopped
Flour   2 tablespoons
Sugar   ½ teaspoon
Salt   1½ teaspoons
Celery seed   ½ teaspoon
Freshly ground pepper   dash
Water   ¾ cup
Vinegar   ⅓ cup

Cool potatoes, then peel and slice thin. Cook bacon in skillet, then drain on paper. Sauté onion in bacon fat until golden brown. Blend in next 5 ingredients, and cook over low heat, stirring constantly, until bubbly. Remove from heat, stir in water and vinegar, then return to heat and simmer 1 minute. Stir in potatoes and crumbled bacon bits. Remove from heat and serve, or cover until serving time. Serves 6 to 8.

Corn Pudding

From the first permanent English settlement west of the Allegheny Mountains comes this corn pudding. A magnificent example of Kentucky bluegrass country cooking, it is served at the antebellum Beaumont Inn at Harrodsburg, Kentucky, for both lunch and dinner because it is so popular.

Flour   8 tablespoons
Sugar   4 teaspoons
Butter   4 tablespoons, melted
Salt   1 teaspoon
Whole kernel corn   2 cups
Eggs   4, well beaten
Milk   4 cups

Stir together first 5 ingredients. Combine eggs and milk and stir into corn mixture. Pour into a greased 2-quart casserole dish and cover. Place on trivet on stove top and let cook, stirring several times, for 45 to 60 minutes. Serves 8 to 12.
Note: In a conventional oven, bake at 400° for 45 minutes.

Snaps with an "Old Ham Bone"

In the South they still say you can spot a Yankee by the way he cooks his green beans. Cooked for hours with ham and seasonings, the beans should be olive green, tasty, and tender—no crisp Yankee green beans for a "true Southerner."

Ham bone or ham scraps
Water 2 cups
Green beans* 2 pounds
Small red pepper 1, crushed
Salt ½ teaspoon
White pepper to taste
Sugar 1 teaspoon
Vinegar ¼ teaspoon
Small onion 1

Boil ham bone in large saucepan with water. String beans and break into desired lengths. Add beans and remaining ingredients except onion to bone and water. Put onion in middle of beans. Cover and simmer 2 to 3 hours until most of the water has evaporated and the beans are tender. (Add more water, if necessary, before 2 hours have passed.) Remove bone and serve beans. Serves 6 to 8.

* Kentucky Wonder string beans are the best. Blue Lake beans are good, too.

Pennsylvania Red Cabbage

Pennsylvania Dutch cooks were reputed to be the best of their day. Even George Washington turned over his important Mount Vernon kitchen to one, who would have served him this cabbage dish along with Beer-Glazed Sausages, Potato Dumplings, and Lemon Pot Pie (see Index).

Large onion   1, finely chopped
Shortening or bacon drippings   2 tablespoons
Apples   2, peeled, cored, and thinly sliced
Water   1 cup
Red wine vinegar   ½ cup
Sugar   2 tablespoons
Salt   1 teaspoon
Pepper   dash
Bay leaf   1
Red cabbage   1 medium head, shredded
Flour   1 tablespoon

Sauté onion in shortening in heavy pot. Add apples and cook a few minutes. Stir in next 6 ingredients and simmer until blended. Add cabbage and simmer on back of stove top until cabbage is well done. Mix flour with some of the cooking liquid. Stir in and simmer another 30 minutes or more. Serves 6 to 8.

Shaker Spinach

Led by Mother Ann in 1774, the Shakers came to America to practice their religion of simplicity and celibacy. They got their name from intensely emotional worship services that caused them to quiver and shake. In their orderly lives, there was "a place for everything and everything in its place"—a plus in their kitchens because the sisters rotated duties. This vegetable dish was one of their simplest and best.

Green onions   2, with tops, thinly sliced
Butter   2 tablespoons
Fresh spinach   2 pounds, coarsely chopped
Parsley   2 tablespoons chopped
Thyme   ¼ teaspoon
Salt   ¼ teaspoon
Freshly ground pepper   to taste

Sauté onions in butter in saucepan. Add remaining ingredients and simmer in their own liquid until vegetables are limp but still bright green. Serves 6.

"Green Steak"

"As soon as the frogs started croaking in the spring, my ma used to send us younguns looking for wild greens," remembers a southern black woman descended from a South Carolina slave brought from Africa to work on the cotton plantations. "It's the best Spring Tonic you can find... as necessary during the month of April as spring plowing...full of iron and vitamins...good for what ails you..." Wild or fresh from the garden or supermarket, this is how they cook them.

Greens*   1 pound
Bacon   4 strips or
    Fatback   ¼ pound or
    Ham   cooked and chopped and
    Butter   1 tablespoon
Green onions   10, chopped
Salt   ½ teaspoon
Pepper   1 teaspoon
Eggs   2, hard-cooked and chopped
Corn Bread (see Index)

Cover greens with water and simmer 3 to 6 hours. Drain, squeezing out excess moisture. Cook bacon in a heavy pot. Remove small amount of bacon for garnish. Add greens and onions and stir together. Add salt and pepper. Add water to saturate greens, then simmer covered at least 1 hour. Serve garnished with chopped bacon and eggs. Serve the "pot likker" for dipping corn bread.
* Poke salad, dandelion greens, winter cress, and other well-identified wild greens; or commercially grown greens, kale, collards, turnips, or beets.
Note: To soak up excess grease after bacon is added, put a slice of bread on top of the cooking greens. To cut grease, add 1 teaspoon vinegar to the pot.
Variation: Put bunches of greens in heavy pot with water to cover. Add ham, salt pork, or bacon. Put slice of bread on top and add 1 teaspoon vinegar. Simmer all day or all night, depending on your schedule. Stir in a pulverized red pepper and add salt to taste.

Gruyère Cheese Grits

Grits are a delicacy made of corn that has been soaked in the lye leached from wood stove ashes, then dried and ground. Southerners are known for their love of grits at breakfast time. Their secret is to cook the meal long and slow with plenty of liquid and butter. This banquet version accompanies meat as a sure way to convert any Yankee into a grits lover.

Milk 1 quart
Butter ½ cup
Raw grits 1 cup
Gruyère cheese ¼ pound, cubed
Parmesan cheese ½ cup grated
Salt 1 teaspoon
Red pepper ⅛ teaspoon

Boil milk and butter in a saucepan. Stir in grits and simmer covered about 30 minutes until tender. Remove from heat. Stir in Gruyère, half of Parmesan, salt, and red pepper. Pour into a greased 1½-quart baking dish. Place dish on trivet on stove top. Cover with a larger pan to allow space around the baking dish. Let cook about 1 hour until mixture has solidified. Top with remaining Parmesan. Serves 6 to 8.

Plain Grits

A more basic version of the old-time favorite, these grits are as essential to southern breakfast with bacon and eggs as the plate itself.

Water 1 cup
Salt ½ teaspoon
Raw grits ¼ cup
Butter ¼ cup
Salt to taste

Put water and salt in a heavy pot and bring to a boil. Stir in grits and simmer about 30 to 60 minutes until water is absorbed and grits are tender. Stir in butter. Adjust salt to taste. Add more water if necessary to make smooth consistency. Serves 4.

Cowpoke Beans

Three or four million cattle roamed Texas untended in 1865 because men had abandoned them to fight the Civil War. After the conflict the legendary cowboy began the chore of herding cattle from open range up the Chisholm Trail, from the Mexico border to Kansas railheads. From there the cattle were shipped to hungry eastern markets. The "trail bosses" directed the cowboys and animals across hostile land as if they were a military operation. In three years they delivered 1.5 million valuable beasts. By 1890 these heroes on horseback were fenced in by homesteaders and cut off by railroads. But they left us a heritage of jeans, boots, ten-gallon hats, and these beans.

Dried pinto or red beans 1 pound
Water 4 cups
Ham bone 1
Green or red chili 1, finely chopped or
    Cayenne ¼ teaspoon
Large onion 1, chopped
Garlic clove 1, chopped
Oil 1 tablespoon
Fresh tomatoes 4 or
    Tomato sauce 8-ounce can
Parsley ¼ cup chopped
Chili con carne seasoning 1½ tablespoons
Salt 1 teaspoon

Soak beans and cook in water until tender. Add ham bone and chili and boil slowly until beans are soft. Sauté onion and garlic in oil heated in iron skillet. Add tomatoes, parsley, and seasonings. Combine with beans and continue cooking several hours until all ingredients are blended and the liquid is mostly absorbed. Serves 6.

San Fernando Beans

In the mission days, Franciscan friars of the Roman Catholic Church converted many California Indians to Christianity and taught them farming and weaving. Over a fifty-year period, they built a string of missions through southern California, each within a day's walk of the next. The seventeenth mission, founded in 1797 at San Fernando, was known for its hospitality. This recipe from that region is surely similar to the bean pot that was waiting on the stove top for overnight guests to arrive.

Dried kidney beans   1 pound
Water
Bulk sausage   ½ pound
Apples   2 cups sliced
Brown sugar   ¼ cup
Small onions   4, sliced
Salt   3 teaspoons
Pepper   ¼ teaspoon
Dry mustard   1 teaspoon
Sage   ½ teaspoon
Chili powder   ½ teaspoon
Vinegar   2 tablespoons
Green pepper   ½, chopped
Garlic cloves   2, minced
Tomato juice   1½ cups

Soak beans overnight in water, then cook until tender. In Dutch oven, or heavy pot with top, lightly fry sausage. Add remaining ingredients except beans and cook until sauce thickens. Add beans and simmer about 2 hours until beans are blended into sauce, or let sit on low heat part of stove all day. Serves 10.

Boston Baked Beans

When you want to take a day off, follow the example of the Puritan women of seventeenth-century Massachusetts. They baked their beans on Saturday and served them cold with brown bread on Sunday. These protestants who broke away from the Church of England and came to America in 1628 and 1630 to practice simple religion and simple living had to finish their weekly chores by Saturday's sunset. As towns developed, bakers took over the Saturday bean and bread baking to free the women for other chores.

Dried navy beans 2 pounds
Water
Large onion 1, chopped
Molasses 1 cup
Lean salt pork or bacon ½ pound, sliced ¼-inch thick
Dry mustard 1 teaspoon
Salt to taste
Pepper ⅛ teaspoon

Cover beans with water and soak several hours or overnight. Drain beans, cover with fresh water in heavy pot, and cook on low heat part of stove until tender. Add remaining ingredients, pressing pork down into top of beans. Cover and bake slowly on low heat part of stove using trivet under pot. Add water as needed throughout cooking, but let sauce thicken toward end of cooking. Serves 10.

Maple Baked Beans

Maple syrup satisfied the colonist's sweet tooth since cost of imported cane sugar was prohibitive and maple trees grew native in New England. Vermont boasts the purest grade of maple syrup found anywhere. Even today sugar harvesters laboriously process syrup by tapping trees in sloshy snow of early spring and collecting—drip by drip—forty gallons of sap to boil into one gallon of syrup. Then they use it in their beans.

Dried small white beans 1 quart
Water
Salt pork ¼ pound
Pure Vermont maple syrup 1 cup
Salt 1 teaspoon
Pepper ⅛ teaspoon
Dry mustard ¼ teaspoon
Small onion 1, diced
Ginger 1 teaspoon
Boiling water

Soak beans in water several hours and parboil until tender. Place half the beans in a bean pot. Score pork and place on top of beans, then add remaining beans. Mix ½ cup syrup and other ingredients together and pour over beans. Fill pot with boiling water, cover, and cook on stove top for 4 hours. (You may need a trivet.) Remove cover, add remaining syrup, and cook about 30 minutes until beans are tender and gooey. Serves 8 to 10.

Main Dishes

Whether preparing the animal just slaughtered, the game just bagged, or what the butcher had to sell, good cooks have one goal, summed up by cookbook author Annie R. Gregory in 1902: "To be a good cook means the economy of your great grandmother and the science of modern chemists. It means much tasting and no wasting. It means English thoroughness, French art and Arabian hospitality. It means, in fine, that you are to see that everyone has something nice to eat."

Sauerbraten   (Sour Pot Roast)

A Christmas tree in every home is a surprisingly recent phenomenon for America. In England during the Middle Ages Christmas became such a rowdy and boisterous occasion that it was outlawed and Puritans brought the law to Massachusetts. Even until the Civil War, rowdy groups of drunken men caroused the streets on Christmas. But when the German immigrants of the 1800s brought with them their treasured Christmas tree ornaments, the season became what we know today, with decorations, carols, and religious services. They also brought sauerbraten to serve at the festive Yuletide gatherings.

Beef rump or round roast   4 pounds
Dry red wine   1½ cups
Tarragon white wine vinegar   1 cup
Salt   1 teaspoon
Black peppercorns   1 teaspoon
Thyme   ½ teaspoon
Allspice   ⅛ teaspoon
Dry mustard   1 teaspoon
Bay leaves   3
Whole cloves   10
Medium onions   3, sliced
Carrot   1, sliced
Celery   ½ cup, with leaves, chopped
Oil   3 tablespoons
Flour   2 tablespoons
Gingersnaps   5, crumbled
Sour cream   1 cup

Place roast in large bowl. Mix next 12 ingredients and pour over meat. Cover with cheesecloth and marinate in refrigerator for 5 days, turning twice a day. To cook, heat oil in large Dutch oven and brown roast on all sides. Stir flour into oil and gradually add marinade and gingersnaps. Turn meat to coat, then simmer slowly about 3 hours. Just before serving, stir in sour cream. Remove roast to platter and serve thinly sliced. Serves 6.
Note: In a conventional oven, cook at 300° for 2½ hours.

74 *Main Dishes*

Swedish Glottstek

More than a million Swedes who faced land shortages and a population explosion in their own country responded in the 1850s to the American campaign to recruit experienced farmers. They brought with them this recipe, which reflects their love of delicately spiced foods, when they settled Minnesota, upper Mississippi Valley, and New England.

Beef rolled roast   4 pounds
Allspice   ¼ teaspoon
Salt   1 teaspoon
Pepper   ½ teaspoon
Butter   3 tablespoons
Oil   1 tablespoon
Large onions   2, chopped
Flour   3 tablespoons
Water   ¼ cup
Bay leaves   2
Vinegar   2 tablespoons
Molasses   2 tablespoons
Heavy cream   ½ cup

Rub roast with allspice, salt, and pepper. Heat butter and oil in Dutch oven or large heavy pot with cover. Brown roast on both sides and remove from pan. Sauté onions, then add flour and brown it slightly. Stir in water, bay leaves, vinegar, and molasses. Return roast to pot, cover, and simmer 2 to 3 hours until meat is tender. Remove meat from pot and place on platter. Slice thin. Add cream to pan juices to make a sauce. Serve over meat. Serves 10 to 12.

American Roast Beef

Ernest Hemingway, William Faulkner, and others believed that Huckleberry Finn *was the first American novel to be written with an American conscience using American language. The man who wrote it, Mark Twain (born Samuel L. Clemens, 1835–1910), appreciated American food, especially after a long European tour that he found most unappetizing. He sent a menu on a boat ahead of him so his meal would be hot when he got home. This meat was on his list, along with "green corn on the ear" and New Orleans "croakers."*

Suet or oil 4 tablespoons
Rump or lean chuck roast 6 pounds
Salt to taste
Pepper to taste
Water ½ cup
Medium onion 1, sliced
Flour 1 teaspoon (optional)
Water 1 teaspoon (optional)

Heat suet in a cast-iron or heavy kettle on stove top. Brown roast and season with salt and pepper. Add water and onion and cover kettle. If desired, mix flour and water into paste and use to seal lid. Cook about 3½ hours until tender. Serves 12.

Skipperlabskava   (Beef and Potatoes)

An historic favorite of Norwegian sailors, this version of meat and potatoes appeals even when you haven't had too much fish at sea.

Butter 2 tablespoons
Onions 2 large, sliced
Beef chuck 1½ pounds, cut into ¼-inch slices and slightly pounded
Potatoes 6 medium, peeled and thickly sliced
Salt 1½ teaspoons
Pepper ½ teaspoon
Hot water 1½ cups
Beer ¼ cup
Parsley ¼ cup chopped

Heat butter in 6-quart Dutch oven. Sauté onions and brown meat at once. Remove half of mixture. Cover remaining with half the potatoes, half the salt, and half the pepper. Add the half of mixture removed from pan and cover with other half of potatoes, salt, and pepper. Pour water and beer over layers. Cover and place on stove top to cook for 2 hours until meat is tender. Serves 10.
Note: In a conventional oven, bake at 375° for 1 hour.

Four-Layered Dinner

One meat, one pot, one heat characterize this economical recipe from a family of the rural piedmont in South Carolina. Even until the 1930s, just when most people were giving up wood stoves, they cooked with a pot hung over the open fire. Substitute your own choices of meat and vegetables if you wish and stretch the heat from your stove top.

Oil   1 tablespoon
Chuck roast   3 pounds
Rosemary   ¼ teaspoon crushed
Salt and pepper   to taste
New potatoes   6, scrubbed and cut in half
Green beans   2 pounds, strung and cut
Carrots   4, sliced diagonally in chunks
Celery   1 stalk, coarsely chopped
Salt pork or bacon   ¼ pound, chopped (optional)

Put heavy kettle on stove top, add oil, and heat. Brown roast on both sides. Sprinkle with rosemary, salt, and pepper. When roast has cooked about 1½ hours, put potatoes on top of it and sprinkle lightly with salt and pepper. Lay beans over potatoes, carrots over beans, and celery over all. Again sprinkle lightly with salt and pepper. Put pork over vegetables, if desired. Cover pot and cook until vegetables are tender and meat is done. Lift out layers separately to serve. Serves 6 to 8.
Variations: Change basic meat to ham, pork, or chicken. Southerners add okra as the last layer. Choose your own vegetable medley, but keep vegetables separate.

Range Stew

Called the Black Hills because dark lodgepole pine cover their slopes, these mountains jut abruptly from the flat plains of western South Dakota. The hills turned golden in 1874 when an army expedition discovered ore there. The largest gold mine in the country, Homestake Mine, was discovered there by prospectors. But gold lay for European financiers, especially Scots, in the green grazing lands around the hills as well. Rather than gamble in gold, they poured their money into the cattle industry and hit it rich. Grass-fed beef, used originally in this recipe, was tougher than our chemical-injected, corn-fattened beef but was tender when cooked this way.

Lean beef sirloin steak   2 pounds
Potatoes   2 pounds
Rosemary   ½ teaspoon
Salt and pepper   to taste
Parsley   1 tablespoon chopped
Onion   1, sliced
Cold water

Remove fat from beef and cut into serving-size pieces. Cut potatoes into 3 or 4 pieces and lay in bottom of greased 1½-quart baking dish. Sprinkle with seasonings and herbs. Layer meat, then onions. Alternate layers, ending with potatoes, until dish is full. Fill three-fourths full with water. Cover, place on trivet, and cook on stove top about 2 hours. Serves 6.

Cornish Pasties

"Do you have a job for my cousin Jack?" one Cornishman after another asked the mine boss of the Comstock Lode (rich veins of silver and gold at Virginia City, Nevada, claimed in part by Henry J. B. Comstock in 1859). And so hard-rock English miners came to Colorado and California to work the lode mines. With them came Cornish pasties. Each day they carried them down into the mines with their "billy cans" of tea. This meal-in-one is as common today in the Nevada City–Grass Valley area of California as hamburgers are in other American towns.

Pastry dough   for two 9-inch crusts
Chopped round steak   1 pound
Onions   1½ cups chopped
Potatoes   1 cup uncooked and finely diced
Salt and pepper   to taste
Butter or margarine
Parsley   finely chopped
Egg   1, beaten
Heavy cream   ½ to 1 cup

Roll dough out ⅛-inch thick and cut into eight 5-inch circles. Mix together next 4 ingredients and place 2 to 3 tablespoons of mixture on each dough round. Dot with butter and sprinkle with parsley. Moisten edges of dough and fold over. Press edges together with a fork, prick tops, and brush with egg. Place on baking tin, set on trivet on stove top, and cover with larger baking pan. Cook about 1 hour until meat is done. Gently slash the tops and pour 1 to 2 tablespoons of cream into each incision. Continue cooking about 15 minutes until cream is absorbed. Makes 8.
Note: In a conventional oven, bake at 325° for 1 hour.

Stew with Dumplings

The Homestead Act of 1862 gave 160 acres of free land to any person over twenty-one who could improve and live on it for five years. School marm Mary Johnson had come from Iowa with her parents to a Colorado homestead at age thirteen. After she graduated from high school—a little delayed because schools came slowly to the frontier—she homesteaded alone in a two-room cottage near Sterling. At thirty-three she married Horace Linvill and added 160 acres to her original plot. When her husband became seriously ill, she stopped teaching school to care for him. She earned what she could from hatching baby chickens to sell and grew a huge garden. Rabbit and venison were substituted for store-bought meats. Her ladies club often met for potlucks, and Mary brought this tasty stew, now recorded in the archives of the Overland Trail Museum in Sterling, Colorado.

Lean stew beef* 2 pounds, cut into small pieces
Boiling water
Carrots 2 cups sliced
Onions 2 cups chopped
Potatoes 4 cups cut into cubes
Tomatoes 1 cup
Salt 1 tablespoon
Pepper ¼ teaspoon
Dumplings
Flour 1 tablespoon
Parsley 2 tablespoons chopped
Water ¼ cup

Put meat in large pot and cover with boiling water. Cover pot and simmer about 2 hours. Add carrots and onions and simmer 15 minutes. Add potatoes, tomatoes, and seasonings, then add more boiling water to cover vegetables. Simmer about 30 minutes until vegetables are tender. Lift meat and vegetables from the stock with a slotted spoon. Strain stock and reheat in pot. Drop dumplings by spoonfuls into hot stock, then cover kettle and simmer dumplings for 20 minutes. Remove dumplings from stock. Pour off stock and save for later use in soup, leaving two cups in pot. Mix flour with water and add to stock. Simmer 3 minutes and pour over meat and vegetables. Serve with dumplings in flat soup bowl with stew ladled over them and parsley sprinkled over all. Serves 8.
* Or you can use rabbit and suet, half rabbit and half beef, or venison.

Dumplings

Flour 1 cup
Baking powder 2 teaspoons
Salt ½ teaspoon
Shortening 1 teaspoon
Cold water

Sift flour, baking powder, and salt into a bowl. Rub in shortening lightly with fingers. Add just enough water to hold dough together.

Swiss Steak

This slow-cooking dish for tough cuts of beef still bears the name of its originators—the Swiss who settled by groups in our midwestern states from Michigan to Kentucky in the last half of the nineteenth century. One of their most influential members was Louis Agassiz (1807-1873), who laid the foundations for our National Academy of Sciences even during the darkest days of the Civil War. Thanks to the Swiss, American school children study fossils and glaciers—pet projects popularized by Agassiz—and we have this tasty recipe.

Beef round steak 3 pounds
Flour 3 tablespoons
Pepper ½ teaspoon
Salt ½ teaspoon
Oil 1 tablespoon
Medium onions 3, chopped
Garlic cloves 2, minced
Butter 2 tablespoons
Canned tomatoes 2 cups or
    Fresh tomatoes 8, peeled and sliced
Beef Stock (see Index) 2 cups
Mushrooms 1 pound, cleaned, sliced, and sautéed

Cut beef into serving portions. Dredge with flour seasoned with salt and pepper and pound with mallet. Heat oil in Dutch oven, then brown meat on both sides in hot oil. Add onions, garlic, and butter, and stir together. Pour tomatoes and stock over beef. Cover and simmer very slowly about 2 to 3 hours until meat is tender. Add mushrooms just before serving. Serves 6 to 8.

Grillades

Although New Orleans is famous for its culinary delights from bouillabaisse to crème brûlée, this authentic recipe was shared by a friend as her everyday taste of home. Tough meat turns into tender morsels when cooked Creole style.

Beef round steak   2 pounds, ½-inch thick
Oil   1 tablespoon
Flour   1½ tablespoons
Large onion   1, thinly sliced
Tomatoes   2 cups peeled
Green pepper   1, minced
Parsley   1 tablespoon chopped
Garlic clove   1, minced
Salt   to taste
Pepper   to taste
Rice or grits

Cut beef into serving-size pieces. Heat oil in heavy pot with lid, then brown meat on both sides. Remove and set aside. Brown flour in same oil, add onion, and sauté until soft. Stir in remaining ingredients except rice and return meat to pan. Cover and simmer over low heat several hours until tender, adding water if necessary. Serve hot with rice or for breakfast with grits. Serves 6.

Beef Stew

As a statesman, Henry Clay (1777–1852) delayed the Civil War by a number of years, was a treaty-signer of the War of 1812, and influenced the passage of the Missouri Compromise to earn the nickname "The Great Pacificator." As a stock breeder, he pioneered efforts to import pedigreed cattle and brought to America the first Hereford cattle, one of our leading beef producers. The white-faced Hereford came to his Ashland home near Lexington, Kentucky, in 1817 and by 1880 was plentiful for use in this stew recipe of the period.

Beef chuck   1 pound, cubed
Potatoes   3, peeled and halved
Carrots   4, peeled and cut in chunks
Medium onion   1, chopped
Sugar   1 tablespoon

Vinegar   2 tablespoons
Salt and pepper   to taste
Tomato juice   1 cup
Flour   1 teaspoon
Water   1 teaspoon

Put beef on bottom of greased Dutch oven or other pot with tight-fitting lid. Put next 7 ingredients on top of beef. Mix flour and water and seal lid to pot with this paste. Put on stove and cook for at least 5 hours until meat is tender. If stove is extremely hot, put trivet under pot for entire cooking time. Keep on low heat part of stove. Serves 6.

Chili Con Carne

For decades, Mexican American produce pickers have followed fruit and vegetable harvests up and down the West Coast. In 1924, there was a little spot in Portland where they could get a real down-home meal. That chili restaurateur had imported this chili con carne recipe from Mexico for $100. (Serve beans as a side dish but never in the chili itself.)

Paprika   1 tablespoon
Bay leaves   10
Mexican sage or oregano   1 tablespoon
Camelia seed or cumin   1 tablespoon
Short red peppers   8
Large Mexican peppers   4
Chili powder   1 tablespoon
Salt   2 tablespoons
Coarsely ground chili meat   6 pounds
Water

Mix together all ingredients except meat and water in a canning kettle. Add meat, cover with water, and cook in open kettle until water has boiled out. Serve with beans cooked separately. Serves 12 to 15.

Texas Chili

In one of the hottest issues ever to hit the Texas legislature, Congressmen declared chili the state dish in 1977. Aztec Indians of Mexico gave us the word itself, which means "hot pepper," but will not claim the "detestable dish." But Texans still revere their "bowl of red." The true origin of chili is vague. One story has it that pounded dried beef, beef fat, dried chili peppers, and salt were dried into pemmican and packed on the trail by cowboys and gold hunters on their way to California. Boiled in water, the dried meat and chilies were an easy trail meal. Another theory is that chili was invented in San Antonio around 1830 as a cheap dish with bits of meat and equal amounts of peppers. The thing to do on a Saturday night was to eat a bowl of chili downtown. "Chili queens," gaily dressed with roses pinned to their bosoms, hawked chili from large caldrons that simmered over charcoal or mesquite fires as musicians serenaded. The rest of the country heard about chili when a man named Myers took his "San Antonio Chilley Stand" to the Chicago World's Fair in 1890. Despite the controversy, Texas statesmen decided to take official action and called the dish "blessedness."

Coarsely ground chili meat   5 pounds
Sirloin tips   ⅓ pound, diced
Medium onions   3 or 4, chopped
Green peppers   3, minced
Garlic cloves   3, minced
Fresh jalapeño pepper   1, diced, with 6 to 8 seeds or
    Canned jalapeños   half of 4-ounce can
Kidney beans   two 15-ounce cans
Beer   10 ounces
Tomato sauce   two 16-ounce cans
Mushrooms   1½ cups coarsely chopped
Parsley   1½ cups chopped
Stewed tomatoes   27-ounce can
Cumin   1 teaspoon
Mild chili powder   2½ teaspoons
Hot chili powder   2½ teaspoons
Bay leaves   6
Oregano   1 tablespoon
Worcestershire sauce   2 big dashes
Tabasco sauce   2 dashes

Brown meat in large heavy pot. Add next 4 ingredients and sauté. Add remaining ingredients and cook over low heat for 3 hours. Freezes well. Serves 15 to 20.

Old Country Cabbage Balls

Catherine the Great of eighteenth-century Russia promised Germans who would settle in her country religious freedom and immunity from military service. By 1870 these privileges waned in the wake of rising Russian nationalism. Cossacks raided one German family, taking their cows and crops. Left with nothing to eat but frozen cabbages in the field, the father indentured himself to an eastern Washington State wheat farmer and brought his family to America. This recipe is from that family.

Medium cabbage 1
Ground beef 1½ pounds
Medium onion 1, chopped and steamed until soft
Egg 1
Dry bread 3 slices, torn in pieces
Rice 1 cup uncooked
Green pepper 2 tablespoons chopped
Salt pork 4 slices
Water or Beef Stock (see Index) 2 cups
Bay leaves 3
Flour 3 tablespoons

Steam cabbage about 15 minutes until leaves separate. Mix next 6 ingredients, knead well, and form into meatballs. Wrap a cabbage leaf around each meatball. In a skillet sauté salt pork. Add cabbage balls and brown lightly. Add water and bay leaves, then cover and simmer on stove top slowly for 1 hour. Thicken gravy with flour and cook a few minutes longer. Serves 6 to 8.

Polenta

Italian peasants eat this life-sustaining mush soft and hot with milk and honey or hardened and cold with sauces. Since ancient Roman times, they had made it with pearl barley (the grain from which the name comes), ground chestnuts, millet, chick-peas, and wheat. But when they were introduced to American corn by Spanish explorers, they used it as the main ingredient. When Italian immigrants left their war-torn country to come to America, they brought this dish with them. Traditionally it is cooked in a copper pot and stirred until a wooden spoon stands alone.

Coarse yellow cornmeal   1 cup
Cold water   2 cups
Hot water or Chicken Stock (see Index)   3 cups
Salt   1½ teaspoons
Italian Sauce   or
    Milk and honey   or
    Parmesan cheese

Stir cornmeal into cold water in a 1½-quart saucepan until there are no lumps. Add hot water and salt. Place pan on low heat part of stove and simmer an hour, stirring from time to time. When the mixture separates easily from the side of the pan or the spoon stands alone, spread it ½-inch thick on a large oiled wooden bread board to cool and serve with Italian Sauce. Or serve it hot with milk and honey or Parmesan cheese. Serves 6.

Italian Sauce

Oil   3 tablespoons
Large onion   1, chopped
Garlic cloves   3, minced
Ground beef   1 pound
Tomato sauce   three 6-ounce cans
Tomato paste   6-ounce can
Rosemary   1 teaspoon
Bay leaf   1, crushed
Allspice   ½ teaspoon
Parsley   ½ cup minced
Mushrooms   1 cup sliced
Salt and pepper   to taste
Dry red wine   ½ cup

Heat oil in large skillet. Add onion and garlic and cook until soft. Add ground beef and brown. Add remaining ingredients and cook about 6 hours on back of stove.

Cranberry Meatballs

It was undoubtedly a festive occasion when the Pilgrims landed on the bleak, cold shores of Plymouth, Massachusetts, on 26 December 1620. The 102 passengers disembarked from the **Mayflower** *to find our native cranberry ripe and waiting for them. The berries stay on the bushes until spring in the cool, swampy bogs of the Massachusetts coast. Today, the deep red berries are still right for a festive occasion.*

Lean ground beef 1 pound
Bread crumbs ½ cup
Egg 1
Onion 2 tablespoons minced
Salt ½ teaspoon
Pepper ⅛ teaspoon
Butter 1 tablespoon
Jellied cranberry sauce 1 cup
Water ½ cup

Combine first 6 ingredients and form into balls the size of a walnut. Melt butter in skillet and brown meatballs. Mix cranberry sauce with water and pour over meatballs. Tightly cover skillet and cook about 30 minutes. Serves 8.
Variation: Make meatballs cocktail size and cook 15 minutes. Serve with toothpicks for an appetizer straight from the stove top.

Swedish Meatballs

A Swedish city girl joined her sweetheart in the Pennsylvania steel mill district of the early 1900s and perfected this meatball recipe as a new bride. In years to come, she taught her son's bride the fine points of making the meatball—steam the onion first so it will not be bitter, thoroughly knead the meat mixture so it will hold together, and spread meatballs around the pan before you thicken the delicate gravy. The daughter-in-law has passed on the technique to us.

Onion ½ cup chopped
Ground beef 1 pound
Pork sausage ½ pound
Salt 1 teaspoon
Pepper 1 teaspoon
Allspice 1 teaspoon or less to taste
Egg 1
Whole wheat bread 2 slices
Milk about 1 cup
Oil
Flour 1 tablespoon

Steam onion in small amount of water to soften. Drain and mix with next 6 ingredients. Soak bread in water, squeeze as dry as you can, then cut into small pieces. Knead bread into mixture. Add milk until mixture feels tacky and continue to mix ingredients well. Form into walnut-sized balls. Heat a small amount of oil to cover an iron skillet, then brown meatballs. Pour off excess fat, add enough water to cover meatballs, then cook gently 30 to 60 minutes. Thicken gravy with flour. Serves 6.

Kreplach

Persecuted elsewhere in the world, Jews came to America where they could pursue their love of learning and excel in many areas. They brought with them their superb cultural cuisine, which includes this little meat dumpling. Operatic soprano Beverly Sills remembers as her happiest holiday one New Year's Day she spent at her grandmother's home and ate kreplach.

Ground beef ½ pound
Onion ¾ cup chopped
Egg 1, beaten
Salt ½ teaspoon

Egg 1
Water 2 tablespoons
Salt ½ teaspoon
Flour ¾ cup
Chicken Stock (see Index) 2 cups

In skillet, cook beef and onion until tender. Drain fat, stir in 1 beaten egg and salt, and cool. Make dough by mixing another egg, water, and salt with enough flour to make moderately stiff dough. Roll out and cut into 2-inch squares. Place 1 teaspoon cool filling on each square. Moisten edges, fold diagonally, then seal. Simmer stock in saucepan. Drop in dumplings and cook about 15 minutes until tender. Serves 4.

Hamburger and Corn Hot Dish

Laura Ingalls Wilder preserved for today's children the sensations of pioneer life—moving endless miles across a prairie sea, lifting log upon log to build a home, scaring blackbirds away from a cornfield. In the great American westward migration, her own family backtracked after some despair in Indian territory, and settled in the little town of Burr Oak, Iowa. Her father and mother ran a hotel there and nine-year-old Laura took the cows to pasture, wandered in cool, green cornfields, and washed in a tin basin before eating this dish, which was cooked by many of her neighbors in that Iowa region. Express your own pioneer spirit and add your favorite herbs and spices to this basic recipe.

Lean ground beef 1 pound
Medium onion 1, chopped
Frozen corn 10-ounce package
Macaroni 1 cup uncooked
Chicken Stock (see Index) 1½ cups
Flour 2 tablespoons
Butter 2 tablespoons
Milk 2 cups
Salt and pepper to taste

Place heavy pot on hot spot of stove. Put in meat and onion and brown. Stir in remaining ingredients, cover pot, and place on trivet. Cook on stove top several hours until liquid is absorbed, stirring occasionally. Serves 6 to 8.
Note: In a conventional oven, cook at 350° for 1 hour.

Hum Bow (Chinese Steamed Buns)

Chinese emigrants came to California in 1849 along with other fortune seekers. In the womanless society of the gold fields, they struck pay dirt with a wash tub and a stew pot. On American soil they invented chop suey and chow mein to feed hungry miners in cheap quantities. But for their own fare they preferred these delicate dumplings.

Dry yeast 4 teaspoons
Warm water ½ cup
Salt 1 tablespoon
Lukewarm water 2 cups
Flour 7 to 7½ cups
Filling
Mayonnaise and hot mustard garnish or
    Catsup garnish

Dissolve yeast in warm water and let set 10 minutes or until it becomes active. Add salt, lukewarm water, and 2 cups flour to yeast and beat. Gradually add remaining flour and knead about 10 minutes. Allow to double its bulk. Roll out into rounds and let rise again. Place 2 tablespoons filling in center of each round. Fold up sides to meet in center and press edges together. Place steamer rack over boiling water in large pot or place disposable aluminum pan with holes punched in it on rack and tilt to one side. Place buns in pan and steam 20 to 25 minutes. Remove from kettle, cool, and serve with mayonnaise and hot mustard. Serves 12.

Filling

Onion 1 cup chopped
Cabbage 3 cups shredded
Ground beef ½ pound

Sauté onion and cabbage. Add beef and cook until done.

Mount Vernon Baked Short Ribs

It is a wonder that George Washington (1732-1799) had time to be "Father of the Country," command the Continental Army, and help write the United States Constitution, for his Mount Vernon home was what he called a "well resorted tavern." The stream of guests was so constant that in twenty years he and Martha seldom had dinner alone. He must have been an armchair chef, too, for this recipe was recorded in his own handwriting.

Flour 4 tablespoons
Salt 1 teaspoon
Pepper ¼ teaspoon
Beef short ribs 4 pounds
Butter 2 tablespoons
Medium onions 3, chopped
Brown sugar 2 tablespoons
Vinegar 1 tablespoon
Dry mustard ½ teaspoon
Catsup ½ cup
Bottled ale or beer ½ cup
Beef Stock (see Index) 1 cup
Carrots 6, peeled and halved

Combine flour, salt, and pepper, then roll ribs in mixture. Heat butter in skillet and brown ribs on all sides. Add onions and sauté. Combine next 6 ingredients, add to skillet, cover tightly, and cook 1½ to 2 hours. Add carrots and cook another hour. Serves 6.
Note: In a conventional oven, cook at 350° for 1½ hours, add carrots, and cook for another hour.

Red Flannel Hash

Ethan Allen's Green Mountain Boys fought to make Vermont the fourteenth state of the Union in 1791. To keep up their strength, they chowed down on this hash made with leftover corned beef.

Medium onion 1, finely diced
Butter 2 tablespoons
Leftover boiled corned beef 1 pound, with some fat, diced
Potatoes 2 cups cooked and diced
Beets 2 cups cooked and diced
Heavy cream 2 tablespoons
Salt ½ teaspoon
Pepper to taste

Sauté onion in butter until tender. Toss remaining ingredients and spread evenly in skillet. Cover and cook on stove top until bottom of hash is crusty. Serves 6.

90 Main Dishes

Corned Beef

In the prefreezer era, beef was preserved in "corns of salt" to produce "corned beef." We have never given it up—even after enterprising New Englanders quarried ice from frozen lakes and shipped it in sawdust and Dr. John Gorrie of New Orleans built the first compressed-air refrigeration machine so we could keep meat fresh longer.

Corned beef 3½ pounds
Water
Large onion 1
Whole cloves 4
Bay leaf 1
White vinegar 1 tablespoon
Celery 1 stalk chopped
Brown sugar ¼ cup
French mustard 1 tablespoon
Carrots 5, peeled
Large potatoes 4, peeled
Cabbage small head, cut in wedges
Cooked beets 10 to 12

Put meat in large pot and cover with water. Stud onion with cloves and add to pan with bay leaf, vinegar, and celery. Cover pot and cook gently on stove top 2 to 3 hours. Remove meat and coat with mixture of brown sugar and mustard. Put on a heat-proof platter, set on trivet, cover with roasting pan, and let sit until you cook vegetables. To stock add carrots and potatoes and cook 30 minutes or until tender. Add cabbage and cook 10 minutes. Remove vegetables from pot and put around corned beef on platter along with beets. Serves 6 to 8.

Veal Loaf

My grandmother, Jessie Turner Pritchard, gave up her dream of becoming a concert pianist to rear her five children—and many more who needed her nurture. Even her husband's financial reverses and the Depression didn't stop her from putting another plate on the table if someone "happened" in at mealtime. She shared some of her secrets with me. "Add a little more water to the soup to serve more people." "Spread the grits out on the plate so it looks like more." I suspect her veal loaf was sometimes more cracker than veal, but the genuine love with which she served it kept the crowds coming by at mealtimes.

Veal 3 pounds, ground
Pork ¾ pound, ground
Crackers ¼ cup finely crushed
Eggs 2
Pepper ⅛ teaspoon
Salt ½ teaspoon

Mix together the veal, pork, and half the crackers. Add eggs, pepper, and salt, and mix together. Press into 5 by 9-inch bread pan. Sprinkle remaining crackers on top of meat. Place on trivet on stove top. Cover with inverted roasting pan. Bake about 2 hours until meat is done. Serves 8 to 10.
Note: In a conventional oven, bake at 350° for 1½ hours.

Bewitched Liver

Back in the days when meat did not come in plastic trays covered with cellophane, cooks used every part of an animal—the heart, tongue, lungs, and liver. They "bewitched" less appetizing parts, as in this recipe from the Old South, into tasty, nutritional dishes.

Calf, pork, or veal liver 3 pounds, ground
Bread crumbs 1 cup grated
Eggs 2, well beaten
Salt pork ¼ pound, ground
Salt 2 teaspoons
Black pepper 2 teaspoons
Red pepper ½ teaspoon

Mix all ingredients together and put into a greased 1½-quart mold or casserole dish. Put on rack in large kettle with 1½ inches of water on the bottom. Let steam about 2 hours on low heat part of stove. Remove from kettle and place in cool place. Unmold when thoroughly cold. Serves 6.

Creole Liver

Louisiana lore claims that the first American cooking school was held in New Orleans for French wives and dowered "casket girls" (single women imported as wives for lonely men). The New World larder so offended these women that they threatened to sail home on the next ship. But the governor's cook saved the city when she invited the homesick women to bring their wooden spoons and iron pots to her kitchen to learn some lessons. She had studied the Indian's culinary tricks and substituted local turtles and pigeons for plump French chickens and suckling pigs. This liver dish shows the magic she used to quell the women's rebellion.

Bacon 4 strips, diced
Beef liver 1 pound, sliced ¼-inch thick
Flour 3 tablespoons
Green pepper ⅓ cup diced
Canned tomatoes 2½ cups
Cayenne ⅛ teaspoon
Salt 1½ teaspoons
Chili powder ⅛ teaspoon

Cook bacon in skillet, then push aside in pan. Dredge liver with flour and brown in the same pan. Add remaining ingredients, cover skillet, and simmer 45 minutes. Serves 4.

Pickled Tongue

When a self-sufficient farm family butchered a cow in the old days, every scrap was valued for food. Lungs, heart, tongue—even the blood, which was cooked into pudding—fortified the family members with healthy "constitutions." One country lady, so adept that she could identify a cut of beef by touch, taught her daughter to cook this dish. It will convert any tongue skeptic, especially when it is eaten as a cold cut with potato salad or cottage cheese.

Whole tongue 1
Water
Bay leaf 1
Pickling spices 1 tablespoon
Large onion 1, thinly sliced
Vinegar 1 cup
Water ¾ cup
Pickling spices 1 tablespoon

Cover tongue with water in a large kettle and add bay leaf and 1 tablespoon pickling spices. Place kettle on stove top and boil tongue about 3 hours until tender. Remove from stove top and cool in broth. Remove from broth and peel skin off tongue and remove small bones at the base. Remove fat from broth. Slice tongue and layer in a bowl with onion. Heat together in a saucepan the vinegar, ¾ cup water, and 1 tablespoon pickling spices. Pour mixture over tongue and onion. Cover and let cool overnight. Serves 8.

Note: Beef heart can be treated the same way except that a tablespoon of oil should be added to the initial boiling water.

Irish Lamb Stew

Their hearts were heavy but their stomachs were empty so three and a half million Irishmen left their "Emerald Isle" between 1820 and 1880 to take refuge in America. With "the cold smell of potato mould" (as Seamus Heaney wrote in "Diggings") still in their nostrils, they worked hard in America to build our railroads and mine our coal. And so along with their potatoes, they even could afford to add a hunk of lamb to their stew, which only the wealthy could do back in Ireland.

Lamb shoulder   2 pounds boned, and cut into 2-inch cubes
Cabbage   ¼ small head, shredded (optional)
Leeks   2, sliced
Medium onions   2, sliced
Celery   1 stalk, with leaves, chopped
Carrots   4, peeled and sliced
Medium potatoes   3, peeled and quartered
Salt   1½ teaspoons
Pepper   ¼ teaspoon
Bay leaf   1
Thyme   ¼ teaspoon
Parsley   2 tablespoons chopped
Water

Layer lamb and vegetables in a 2-quart casserole. Season with salt and pepper, and herbs, and cover with water. Cover casserole, set on trivet, and simmer 3 or 4 hours. Serves 6.

Moussaka à la Grecque

Sponge beds and bountiful fishing off the west coast of Florida attracted a sizable community of Greeks to Tarpon Springs at the turn of the century. Among the recipes handed down from mother to daughter in that community, this classic casserole is well worth a little extra trouble.

Large eggplants   2, unpeeled
Salt   1 tablespoon
Olive oil   ¼ cup
Large onions   2, thinly sliced
Mushrooms   ½ pound, thinly sliced
Olive oil   2 tablespoons if needed
Garlic cloves   2, crushed
Shoulder of lamb or beef   2 pounds ground
Olive oil   ¼ cup
Tomatoes   two 16-ounce cans, drained and peeled
Salt   ½ teaspoon
Pepper   ¼ teaspoon
Oregano   ¼ teaspoon
Custard

Assemble this dish in the kitchen and carry it to the stove top to cook. First, slice eggplant into ½-inch circles, spread them out, and sprinkle with 1 tablespoon salt. Let stand for 30 minutes and wipe off excess water with a paper towel. Heat ¼ cup olive oil in skillet and brown eggplant on both sides. Remove eggplant from skillet. Add onions and mushrooms, and the 2 tablespoons of oil, if needed for sautéing. Add garlic and sauté a few more minutes. Remove mixture from skillet. Sauté lamb in additional ¼ cup olive oil. Assemble in greased 2-quart casserole with a layer of one-third of the eggplant, meat, onion-mushroom-garlic mixture, then tomatoes. Sprinkle each layer with salt, pepper, and oregano. Layer 2 more times until all ingredients are used. Place on trivet on stove top. Tightly cover dish and let cook about an hour until all ingredients are cooked through. With 2 forks, make a 3-inch hole in the center of the moussaka. Pour in custard. Cover and cook about 30 minutes until custard is set. Serves 6.
Note: In a conventional oven, bake at 375° for 1 hour.

Custard

Eggs 2
Evaporated milk ½ cup
Yogurt ¼ cup
Lemon rind 1 teaspoon grated
Parsley 2 teaspoons minced
Salt ¼ teaspoon
Pepper pinch

Beat first 3 ingredients together. Add remaining ingredients and mix well.

Pork Chops with Brown Rice

Pigs first rooted around in American ground after Spanish explorer Hernando DeSoto brought them into Florida with his gold-hunting entourage in 1739. Some of these first pigs were given to Indian tribes, and others wandered into the woods when DeSoto and his men left camp to explore and stumbled, incidentally, onto the Mississippi River.

Pork chops 6
Oil 2 tablespoons
Large onion 1, chopped
Brown rice 1 cup uncooked
Worcestershire sauce 2 teaspoons
Parsley 1 tablespoon chopped
Salt ½ teaspoon
Freshly ground pepper ½ teaspoon
Tomatoes 2 cups with juice
Green pepper 1, sliced in rings

Brown chops in oil and set chops aside. Sauté onion in same pan, then mix with next 6 ingredients. Place in casserole with tight-fitting lid. Put green pepper on top of rice mixture, then put chops on top of pepper slices. Cover, place on low heat part of stove, and simmer about 1½ to 2 hours until done. Serves 4 to 6.
Note: In a conventional oven, bake at 350° for 1 hour.

Colonial Pork Chops

In the dense woods of the New World, pigs awaited arrival of the settlers. When preserved by salting, pork was a staple food for these folk and later accompanied pioneers on the westward movement. "Meat" to them meant pork. A butchering day was the only time they could enjoy this fresh pork dish.

Apples   6, peeled, cored, and sliced
Large onion   1, sliced
Salt and pepper   to taste
Butter or margarine   2 tablespoons
Flour   2 tablespoons
Beer   1 cup
Pork chops   4, trimmed

Combine apples, onion, and seasonings in buttered casserole. In a saucepan, melt butter, stir in flour, then add beer and continue stirring until thickened. Put chops over apples and onions, and pour sauce over all. Place casserole on trivet on stove top. Cover and let cook about 2 hours until chops are tender. Serves 4.
Note: In a conventional oven, bake at 350° for 1½ hours.

Sauterne Pork Chops

This is a good wintertime dish embellished with the winter store of fruits from the California wine country.

Medium-thick pork chops   4
Flour   ¼ cup
Oil   1 tablespoon
Salt   1 teaspoon
Pepper   ¼ teaspoon
Sauterne or any white dinner wine   ¼ cup
Apple jelly   ¼ cup

Dredge chops in flour. Heat skillet on stove top and put in oil. Brown chops in skillet on both sides. Put remaining ingredients over chops. Cover pan, set on trivet on stove top, and cook about an hour until chops are tender. Serves 4.
Note: In a conventional oven, cook at 350° for 1 hour.

Sweet and Sour Pork

A golden spike driven into a cross-tie at Ogden, Utah, by Central Pacific and Union Pacific railroad officials marked the meeting of East and West in 1869. Chinese immigrants made up nine thousand of the ten thousand men who built the western half of the span. They proved to be excellent workers and earned their rightful place in American heritage in other fields, also. This dish, as well as its variations, is one of the finest they have added to our cuisine.

Brown sugar 1½ cups
Wine vinegar 6 tablespoons
Tomato sauce 4 tablespoons
Pineapple chunks with juice 20-ounce can
Water or stock (see Index) ⅔ cup
Green pepper 1, cut into inch squares
Cornstarch 3½ tablespoons
Water 4 tablespoons
Tomatoes 2, peeled and cut into inch squares (optional)
Pork* 3 to 4 pounds cut into 1-inch cubes

Mix first 5 ingredients in saucepan and stir. Add green pepper and cook until tender. Mix cornstarch and 4 tablespoons water together, and stir into mixture. Cook until mixture thickens. Add tomatoes just before serving, if desired. Lightly fry pork in separate pan. Remove when done. Pour sauce over it and let simmer until flavors are blended. Serves 6 to 8.
* Beef ribs, shrimp, or chicken are equally good.

Posole

Indians had occupied southwestern North America for thousands of years when Spanish explorers came seeking fabled riches and gold in the 1500s. They were followed by Catholic priests and Spanish colonists, who merged their cuisine of domesticated pork and beef with the Indians' in dishes of peppers and corn in such recipes as this. Today New Mexicans eat posole with a chili stew on Christmas Eve.

Hominy 2½ pounds
Water 1 quart
Pork or beef 2 pounds, cubed
Onion 1, chopped
New Mexican red chili pods 3 to 5
Peppercorns 3 to 5
Oregano 1 tablespoon

Cook hominy in water about 2 to 4 hours (or less if using canned hominy) until tender. Add remaining ingredients and cook about 4 hours until ingredients are blended and creamy. Serves 6 to 8.

Bacon Gravy

Mexican furs, gold, silver, and pack horses lumbered over the Santa Fe Trail—from New Mexico to Independence, Missouri—in the late 1860s. American manufactured goods packed down the trail to New Mexico. Two cultures merged because of this trading along a trail that was one of the longest commercial routes—780 miles—in the prerailroad era. The United States Army hovered close at hand to protect valuable cargo moving at the rate of five thousand wagons a year at the trail's peak use. Both traders and army units ate this bacon smothered in gravy. Since pigs of that era were a leaner breed than ours, use the leanest bacon you can buy.

Lean bacon or lean salt pork 2 pounds sliced
Onion 1, diced
Water 2 cups
Flour 4 tablespoons
"Army Bisquits" (see Index) 6

Chop bacon and stir-fry with onions in skillet. Drain grease and reserve for use in "Army Bisquits." Add water and stir in flour. Return to heat and let cook until mixture thickens and bubbles. Serves 6.

Cowboy Stew

On the cowboy frontier, the chuck wagon cook was second in importance to the trail boss. He was up at three in the morning to start breakfast and went to bed after midnight when the last cup of coffee had been consumed. Since cowboys traveled on their stomachs, the cook had to plan and ration his groceries carefully to last the trip. One bad meal and the hungry cowpokes let him know it. But he heard no complaints when he served this dish.

Bacon ¼ pound sliced, cut in ½-inch pieces
Large potatoes 2, peeled and sliced
Medium onions 2, sliced
Water 5 cups
Salt 1 teaspoon
Bell pepper 1, chopped (optional)

Put bacon in skillet over hot spot on stove and lightly fry. Add next 5 ingredients, cover tightly, and simmer until all ingredients are mushed together. Serves 4 to 6.

Red Beans and Rice

Everybody in Louisiana eats this whether they are Creoles descended from the aristocratic French and Spanish colonists, or Cajuns descended from the French Canadians (Acadians) who took refuge there after the British deported them from Nova Scotia in 1755, or blacks descended from the Negro slaves who came from Africa and became the backbone of southern agriculture. Restaurants and residents traditionally cook red beans and rice on Monday to use Sunday's leftover ham bone.

Dried red beans   2 cups
Water   4 cups
Salt pork   ¼ pound, cut up or
   Sausage   ½ pound or
   Ham bone   boiled and stripped and
   Oil   1 tablespoon
Onions   1 cup chopped or
   Green onions   8 to 10, diced
Garlic cloves   1 or 2, minced
Bell pepper   1, chopped
Flour   1 tablespoon
Tomatoes   2 cups
Salt   1 teaspoon or to taste
Red pepper sauce   1 teaspoon
Cumin   1 teaspoon
Tomato sauce   ½ cup
Chili powder   1 teaspoon
Parsley   1 tablespoon chopped
Rice   4 cups cooked

Soak beans overnight in water. In a large kettle, cook beans on stove top until tender and drain. In a large heavy pot, brown pork (or sauté ham in oil). Add next 4 ingredients and stir to make a roux. Add next 6 ingredients, plus drained beans. Cover and simmer several hours until flavors are blended. Add water while cooking if mixture seems dry. Garnish with parsley and serve on hot rice. Serves 6 to 8.

Hoppin John

According to southern superstition, you must eat this dish on New Year's Day to have good luck in the form of metal coins. For better luck—greenbacks—eat leafy greens along with the peas. The dish's name reflects southern hospitality. When you have unexpected guests you can say, "Hop in, John," if you have a big pot of peas and rice on your stove top. If you also have corn bread, slow-cooked greens, and a sweet pie, that's even better.

Dried black-eyed peas   2 cups
Water   6 cups
Meaty ham hocks   1 pound
Onions   1 cup chopped
Dried red chili   ¼ teaspoon or to taste
Rice   1½ cups uncooked
Salt and pepper   to taste
Green pepper   minced, garnish

Combine peas and water and soak several hours or overnight. Add ham hocks, onions, and chili. Cover and simmer about 2 hours until peas are tender. Remove ham hocks. Cut meat into small pieces and return to pot. Stir in rice, cover, and simmer on back of stove until rice is tender. Remove excess liquid if necessary. Add salt and pepper. Garnish with green pepper just before serving. Serves 8 to 10.

Schnitz und Knepp

*A rare old dish that Mother made that filled
us all with pep,
This generation knows it not—we call it
Schnitz and Knepp*

A Mennonite Brethren woman of German origin recommended this as the tastiest of her heritage foods.

Dried apples 2 cups
Water
Ham 1½ pounds, cut in chunks
Brown sugar 1 tablespoon
Flour 1 cup
Baking powder 2 teaspoons
Salt ½ teaspoon
Pepper ⅛ teaspoon
Egg 1, well beaten
Butter 2 tablespoons, melted
Milk ¼ cup

Cover apples with water and soak overnight. When ready to prepare dish, cover ham with water in kettle and simmer about 2 hours. Add apples and soaking water and continue to simmer about 1 hour until apples are tender, then add sugar. Prepare dumplings by sifting dry ingredients together. Blend egg, butter, and milk and stir into dry ingredients all at once. Drop by tablespoonfuls onto simmering ham and apples. Tightly cover kettle and cook about 20 to 30 minutes until dumplings are done through. Serves 4 to 6.

Boiled Ham

"Hogs eat their fill of raisins and dates...and drink from ditches flowing with wine," wrote early American immigrants in letters to their friends and relatives in meager cottages throughout Europe. These "American letters" were a literature of the unlettered, but they generated a tidal wave of immigrants that swept across America after 1830. The following way of cooking a hog made it tender—even if it hadn't been tenderized by drinking wine from ditches.

Ham 8 to 10 pounds
Water 2 quarts
Cider 1 quart
Mustard 1 tablespoon
Sugar 2 tablespoons
Cracker crumbs

Wash ham and place it skin side down in a large kettle. Cover with water and cider and simmer 20 minutes to the pound. When well done, remove from liquid. Mix mustard and sugar together. Spread all over ham, then roll in cracker crumbs. Put on rack in Dutch oven or covered roasting pan. Let sit on stove top until ham is nicely glazed.

Paste

Recipes were a common language for the Norwegian and English women who settled side by side in Decorah, Iowa, in 1849. They exchanged delicate Norwegian cookies for "Yankee" baked beans and potato salad to create a neighborly bond. One Norwegian-American got this economical leftover idea from her English neighbors before she moved from Wisconsin to northeast Iowa.

Potatoes 4 cups diced
Carrots 1 cup chopped
Onions 1 cup diced
Leftover meat 1 cup finely chopped
Salt to taste
Pepper to taste
Pie crust 1, prepared

Mix together potatoes, carrots, onions, meat, salt, and pepper. Put into greased 8-inch square cake pan. Cover tightly with pie crust. Place on trivet on stove top and cover with inverted baking pan. Cook about 2 hours until it feels done when pierced through with a fork. Serves 6.
Note: In a conventional oven, bake at 350° for 1 hour.

104   Main Dishes

Country Kraut

French frills hit the American frontier when refugees from the French Revolution built a town fit for their queen in the backwoods along the Susquehanna River. The town of "Alizum" had a marketplace, two-story log homes—a three-story cabin for the queen—all with large French windows and metal-hinged shutters that were painted black with white trim. The French refugees transplanted weeping willows, planted flowers, and pruned the river trees for a better view. They drank coffee from fine china cups and ate their "strange" bread possibly with main dishes like this old classic kraut specialty from the Rhineland. One winter after the river thawed, the settlers learned that their queen had been guillotined. So, when Napoleon Bonaparte offered them amnesty in 1803, they quickly abandoned their 10-year project and left for their beloved homeland.

Sausage   1 pound smoked, Polish or other
Chicken Stock (see Index)   1 cup
White wine   ½ cup
Potatoes   2 large, halved and sliced lengthwise
Carrots   4, cut in diagonals
Sauerkraut   10-ounce can, drained

Place sausage in 2-quart baking dish and cover with stock and wine. Add potatoes and carrots. Cover dish with foil. Place on trivet on stove top. Bake 1½ hours. Remove foil. Put sauerkraut in center of sausage. Cover again with foil and cook about 30 minutes longer. Serves 8.
Note: In a conventional oven, bake at 350° for 1 hour. Add sauerkraut and bake 20 minutes longer.

Lentils with Polish Sausage

Serve this Polish dish on Pulaski Day, 11 October, declared by Congress to honor Count Casimir Pulaski. This Polish soldier became commander of the Pulaski's Legion of the United States Cavalry and Light Infantry during the American Revolution. He gave his life for our country and became a national hero for future generations of Polish Americans. Although their presence is recorded in colonial Virginia as makers of "pitch, tar and potash," it was between 1860 and World War I that the major influx of three million arrived. They have shared with us such favorite foods as kielbasa, the sausage used in this lentil dish.

Lentils   1 pound
Cold water
Oil   2 tablespoons
Onions   3, chopped
Garlic cloves   3, minced
Tomatoes   16-ounce can
Tomato sauce   8-ounce can
Kielbasa*   1 pound, cut into thin rounds
Salt and pepper   to taste
Hot water

Cover lentils with cold water and simmer about 20 to 60 minutes until tender. In a heavy kettle, heat oil and sauté onions. Add next 5 ingredients and lentils. Cover, place over low heat part of stove, and cook slowly for about 1 hour, adding hot water from teakettle as needed. Remove lid and cook slowly until liquid reduces and sauce is quite thick. Serves 6.
* Polish sausage

Beer-Glazed Sausages

Beer made of barley, corn, and rice filled Americans' mugs as soon as they could set up breweries in the colonies. Among our prominent brewing forefathers was Samuel Adams, father of the American Revolution. As in this old German recipe, beer was also used in cooking to improve flavor and texture of tough meats and wild game.

Pork sausages
Boiling water
Beer

Pierce sausage casings. Place sausages in saucepan and cover with water from teakettle. Simmer about 30 minutes. Drain liquid, add beer to cover, and cook slowly, turning sausages occasionally, until most of beer evaporates.

Wild Game

A family on the frontier of the East or West could almost starve while the head of the family took his rifle and ventured out into unknown wilderness to shoot whatever game roamed there. Today many of the men who venture into our remaining wilderness to hunt for sport, campaign to conserve our natural resources. National Hunting and Fishing Day (the last Saturday in September) finds duck calling and other exhibits of the sport in shopping center parking lots to encourage conservation of our wilderness heritage. Recipes that follow are to help you cook the game you bag in the wilderness —or the supermarket—on a wood stove.

Braised Venison

Waterways were the chief means of transporting goods and people in early America. Built by government and tradesmen, canals extended natural rivers, and water traffic flourished in the Canal Era until the railroad replaced it in 1860. On the Ohio and Erie Canal, built between 1825 and 1832 to connect Cleveland and Portsmouth, horses and mules trod the two paths pulling boats up and down the canal. About midway on the canal at Coshocton, Ohio, was the finely furnished home of Dr. Maro Johnson, where this indigenous braised venison dish was served.

Venison shoulder (or lean beef)   3 pounds boned
Salt pork   ⅛ pound
Flour   3 tablespoons
Salt   ½ teaspoon
Pepper   to taste
Cooking oil   3 tablespoons
Water   ¼ cup
Vinegar   1 tablespoon
Celery   ¼ cup diced
Onion   ¼ cup minced
Carrot   1 small, pared
Tart apple   1, pared and chopped
Lemon juice   1½ teaspoons

Wipe venison with a damp cloth. Place strips of salt pork down center of venison and roll up from narrow end. Tie securely with cotton string. Dredge venison in mixture of flour, salt, and pepper. Heat oil in Dutch oven and brown venison on all sides. Place on trivet inside the Dutch oven. Add water and vinegar. Cover and simmer on stove top for about 2 hours. Add remaining ingredients, cover, and cook for 1 hour until tender. Serve hot with gravy from cooking. Serves 8.

Hunter's Stew

Beef suet   2 tablespoons
Venison   2 pounds, cut into chunks
Salt and pepper   to taste
Water
Carrots   6, peeled and cut in chunks
Celery   3 stalks, cut in chunks
Medium onions   3, quartered
Potatoes   2, quartered
Tomatoes   28-ounce can

Brown suet in a large skillet. Add meat seasoned with salt and pepper into the pot and cover with water. Cook about 45 minutes until meat is tender. Add remaining ingredients and simmer until all are done. Serves 6 to 8.

Rabbit Pot au Feu

Rabbits   2, 2 to 3 pounds each
Chicken Stock (see Index)   1 quart
Water   1 quart
Red or white wine   2 cups
Salt   1 tablespoon
Bouquet garni*   1, tied in cheesecloth
Fresh baby peas   2 cups shelled or
   Frozen baby peas   10-ounce package
Whole baby carrots   24
Celery   3 stalks, cut in ½-inch slices
Large leeks   3, cut in ½-inch slices
Baby white onions   24
Fresh dill   3 sprigs, coarsely cut up

Dress rabbits and cut into serving-sized pieces. Place in Dutch oven and add next 5 ingedients. Boil, skimming surface to keep liquid clear. Simmer covered on stove top about 1 hour until rabbit is almost tender. Add remaining ingredients and continue simmering about 30 more minutes until vegetables are tender. Remove bouquet garni and lift rabbit and vegetables onto platter. Serve broth separately. Serves 6.
* You can use 1 bay leaf, ¼ teaspoon thyme, 3 cloves, and 4 sprigs parsley.

Swiss Rabbit

A food shortage during the winter of 1857 hit a "very small clearing" in the Michigan woods that was inhabited by fifteen to twenty people. Even though flour soared to five dollars a barrel, the settlers survived. Wild animals were plentiful in the surrounding woods, and the friendly Chippewa Indians helped the settlers kill these animals for meat. That small clearing later became Big Rapids, Michigan, where the Home Economics Extension Club of Mecosta County found this rabbit recipe a handy one to have when times got rough again in 1930.

Rabbit 1, cut in serving portions
Flour ½ to 1 cup
Salt and pepper to taste
Butter 4 tablespoons
Onion 1 small, chopped
Tomatoes 1 cup, canned or fresh
Hot water 1 cup

Roll rabbit pieces in mixture of flour and salt and pepper. Melt butter in skillet on stove top. Put onions and rabbit in melted butter and brown on both sides. Add tomatoes and water. Cover skillet and cook on stove top 2 to 3 hours until done. Add more water if needed as rabbit cooks. Serves 4 to 6.

Rabbit Oswego

Rabbits 2, 2 to 3 pounds each
Salt and pepper to taste
Olive oil 1 cup
Salt pork ½ pound cubed
Garlic cloves 2, sliced
Oregano ½ teaspoon
Celery 1 bunch, tops only

Dress rabbits and cut into serving-sized pieces. Dry and rub with salt and pepper. Put oil into Dutch oven. Heat and add salt pork and garlic. Remove browned garlic, add rabbit to pot, sprinkle with oregano, and add celery tops. Cover pot and cook slowly about an hour until rabbit is tender. Add water during cooking to keep from drying out. Serves 6.

Pigeon with Peas

Young wild pigeons 4
Salt and pepper to taste
Bacon ½ pound, unsliced and diced
Butter or margarine 2 tablespoons
Fresh baby peas 2 cups shelled
Sugar 1 tablespoon
Small onions 8
Lettuce leaves 8, torn in pieces
Flour 1 tablespoon
Water (optional)

Dress birds, wipe dry, and sprinkle inside and out with salt and pepper. Tie legs together. Put bacon and 1 tablespoon butter in bottom of casserole. Put birds breast side up over this. Place on trivet on stove top and cook until they are tender. In a saucepan, melt 1 tablespoon butter. Add next 3 ingredients, cover, and cook on trivet on stove top about 20 minutes. Put lettuce on a platter. Put pigeons on this with pea mixture around them. Reheat drippings in casserole. Stir in flour. Add water if needed to make light gravy. Pour over pigeons and peas. Serves 4.

Smothered Pheasant

Pheasant 2, 3 to 4 pounds
Flour ¼ cup
Butter ¼ cup
Evaporated milk 13-ounce can
Flour ½ cup
Butter ½ cup melted
Medium Cheddar cheese 1 cup grated
Salt 1 teaspoon
Pepper ¼ teaspoon
Small onions 8, steamed
Mushrooms ½ pound, sliced

Dress pheasant and cut into serving-sized pieces, then coat with ¼ cup flour. Melt ¼ cup butter in shallow baking dish and place pheasant in a single layer in the dish. Place pan on trivet and set on stove top. Cover and simmer about 45 minutes until pheasant is tender. Turn pheasant over and bake another 15 minutes. Drain off excess fat. Mix together next 6 ingredients. Put onions and mushrooms over pheasant. Pour milk mixture over all. Cover dish and let cook another 30 minutes. Serves 6 to 8.
Note: In a conventional oven, cook 30 minutes at 425°, then 15 to 20 minutes at 325°.

Festive Turkey

After the Revolutionary War in the 1700s, our founding fathers settled down to form a government. They chose the bald eagle as a symbol of power, courage, and freedom. Benjamin Franklin objected to the choice of "a bird of bad moral character who like those among men live by sharpening and robbing. He is generally poor and often very lousey (to eat) . . ." He preferred the turkey "as a much more respectable bird, and withal a true original Native of America." But with due credit to Franklin's peers, they did by chance choose a bird of a species that gave male and female equal coloring as adults. Still, there are certain days when the turkey really is our national bird.

Turkey   12 to 14 pounds
Water
Celery   4 stalks, chopped
Salt and pepper   to taste
Poultry seasoning   to taste
Stuffing
Butter   (optional)

Debone turkey with a sharp, heavy knife. Place turkey on cutting board breast side down and cut off tail, wings, and legs. Make a cut lengthwise down backbone. Cutting down a side at a time, follow contour of bones, pulling meat back and scraping meat free of carcass. Cut along outside of flat bone at shoulder blade (A). Cut through thigh joints. Cut down to center of bird. Repeat on other side. Cut through breast cartilage and lift out carcass. Sew up leg and wing holes.

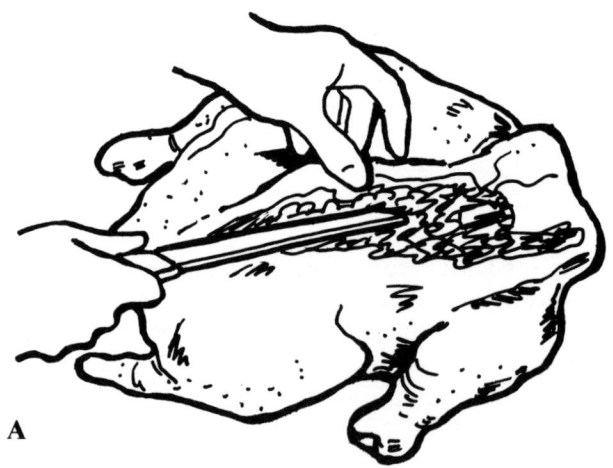

A

Make stock by putting carcass, including tail, wings, and legs, in a large stockpot. Add water to cover carcass by about 2 inches, then add celery and seasonings. Bring to simmer and continue cooking 3 to 4 hours. Remove from heat and cool. Skim off hardened fat, then strain stock through cheesecloth over a sieve.

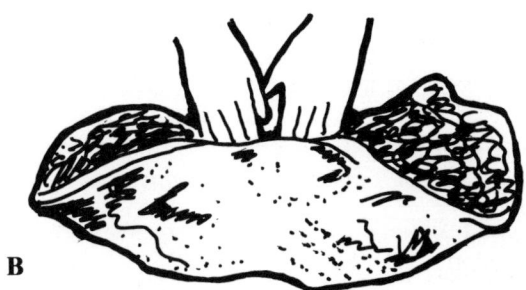

B

Pack stuffing into deboned turkey (B), then roll up bird and stuffing like a jelly roll (C). Wrap in cheesecloth and sew closed. Simmer turkey in stock about 2 hours until meat tests done with a meat thermometer. Remove from stock when cool. Serve cold. Serves 18 to 20.

C

Stuffing

Pork   1 pound, ground
Carrots   4, grated
Bread crumbs   from 4 slices bread
Eggs   3, beaten
Celery   2 stalks, thinly sliced
Orange rind   of 1 orange, grated
Salt   ½ teaspoon
Freshly ground pepper   dash
Parsley   2 tablespoons
Nutmeg   dash
Lemon zest   of 1 lemon
Allspice   ¼ teaspoon

Combine all ingredients.

Braised Duck

Duck 1, 4 to 5 pounds
Flour
Oil 2 tablespoons
Whole cloves 4
Medium onion 1, peeled
Water 2 cups
Dry white wine 1½ cups
Bay leaf 1
Salt 1 teaspoon
Peppercorns 3, crushed
Parsley 3 tablespoons chopped
Rosemary ½ teaspoon crushed

Dress duck and cut into serving-sized pieces, then coat with flour. Heat oil in 2-quart casserole and brown duck on all sides. Stick cloves into onion and add to casserole along with remaining ingredients. Cover and simmer about 2 hours until tender. Serves 4.
Note: In a conventional oven, bake at 350° about 1½ hours.

Kamo Yoshino-Ni   (Duck in Sake Sauce)

California gold glittered just as brightly to Japan as it did to other countries around the world. But the Japanese soon turned from gold to make good use of their innate thrift, efficiency, and foresightedness in farming and fishing. Their success alarmed Caucasians who then passed laws to restrict them. In the Gentleman's Agreement of 1908, Japan denied passports to laborers wanting to work in the United States. The "Ladies' Agreement" thirteen years later ended the import of "picture brides," who had married Japanese American bachelors by proxy. The festering feud exploded twenty years later at Pearl Harbor. In less than forty-eight hours, Japanese Americans, stripped of homes, farms, and businesses, were isolated in relocation centers—a dark period in our history. But Japanese Americans stepped back to share the beauty of their culture in ethnic America. From their cooking vessels comes this savory duck. Serve it with other Japanese dishes or as an entrée with your usual fare.

Whole duck breast 1, boned, with skin on
Salt   to taste
Cornstarch   ¼ cup
Water   2 cups
Sake*   ¼ cup
Chicken Stock (see Index)   1 cup
Sugar   1 teaspoon
Soy sauce   ½ teaspoon
Fresh ginger root   2 teaspoons finely slivered

Slice duck breast diagonally into 16 thin pieces. Salt each piece lightly, then dip each one in cornstarch and shake off excess. Boil 2 cups water in a 1-quart saucepan and add duck slices. When water boils, remove slices with tongs and drain on paper towels. Combine sake and stock in 1½-quart saucepan. Bring to a boil, then stir in sugar, salt, and soy sauce. Add ginger and duck and cook 3 minutes more. Serves 6.
* Rice wine.

Saucy Apple Goose

Pioneers from Iowa and Minnesota moved into South Dakota in 1856 and two years later the Sioux Indians relinquished their land to the white man. Gold and railroads brought more settlers into the Indian territory. The settlers depended on wild game for food and this is one of the ways the pioneer women cooked their geese. This recipe has been relished through the years and preserved for us by the South Dakota Department of Game, Fish, and Parks in Pierre, South Dakota.

Apples   2, peeled, cored, and sliced
Wild goose*   1, dressed
Applesauce   1½ cups
Currant jelly   ¾ cup
Cinnamon   1 teaspoon
Nutmeg   1 teaspoon
Corn syrup   ½ cup

Place apples in goose cavity, then put goose on rack in roasting pan on stove top. Mix remaining ingredients, pour over goose, and cover pan. Cook about 1½ to 2 hours until goose is done, basting throughout cooking. Serve self-made sauce as gravy with carved bird. Serves 4.
* Or tame.
Note: In a conventional oven, bake at 350° for 20 to 25 minutes per pound.

Kylling Med Karve (Chicken and Caraway Seeds)

Norwegian pioneers on the northeast Iowa frontier usually lived in a one-room house with a loft. In summer, they moved the iron wood stove to a nearby shed so they could cook without heating the house. To announce that food was ready and summon the family and guests to table, the cook said, "Vaer sa god" at least three times. Throughout the meal, she repeated the phrase, "Come to the table, help yourself, be so good."

Young hen   1 large, cut into serving-size pieces
Flour   ¼ cup
Salt and pepper   to taste
Shortening   enough to brown chicken
Caraway seeds   2 tablespoons, crushed
Chicken Stock (see Index)   ½ cup
Sour cream   2 cups

Coat chicken in mixture of flour, salt, and pepper. Brown chicken in shortening in cast-iron skillet on stove top. Add seeds, stock, and 1 cup of the sour cream to chicken. Stir gently. Cover and cook 1½ hours until chicken is tender. Just before serving, stir in rest of sour cream. Serves 4.
Note: In a conventional oven, bake at 300° for 1½ hours.

Randolph-Macon Chicken Deluxe

Phi Beta Kappa, *the oldest Greek letter-name fraternity in America, came to be 5 December 1776. The Greek initials mean "Guide of Life," and the society encourages scholarship in the liberal arts and sciences. From the first southern women's college to receive a* Phi Beta Kappa *charter—Randolph-Macon Woman's College—comes this recipe. One of a 93-year-old collection, it is an example of the kind of "brain food" the women students eat, even today, in the college dining room.*

Chipped beef   3-ounce jar dried
Chicken   8 breasts
Bacon   8 slices
Butter   ¼ cup
Sour cream   1 cup
Flour   ¼ cup
Salt   ½ teaspoon
Milk   ½ cup

Line a 9 by 13-inch baking pan with chipped beef. Remove skin from chicken breasts and wrap each with a slice of bacon. Place chicken on top of chipped beef. Slice butter over chicken pieces. In a bowl, mix sour cream, flour, salt, and milk. Pour over chicken. Place pan on trivet on stove top. Cover with inverted roasting pan. Cook about 3 hours. Serves 8.
Note: In a conventional oven, bake at 250° for 3 hours.

Danish Chicken

Mormon missionaries recruited several thousand Danes to populate Salt Lake City in the 1850s. The hard pioneer life drove some of these immigrants back to more settled areas in Iowa, Minnesota, and Wisconsin where they found land more like home and developed fine dairy farms. Butter and cream that smother this chicken remind us of a Danish innovation in America—cooperative creameries. This is how they cooked their chicken on the stove top.

Chicken   1, 3 pounds
Salt and pepper   to taste
Parsley   3 sprigs, chopped
Butter   1 cup
Water   ½ cup
Heavy cream   1 cup
Butter   (optional)

Rub chicken with salt and pepper. Fill cavity with parsley and ½ cup butter. Melt remaining ½ cup butter in large pan with a tight-fitting lid. Brown chicken on all sides. Add water and simmer covered about 1 hour. When chicken is done, add cream (and more butter, if desired) to the liquid in the pan. Serves 4 to 6.

Threshers' Chicken Casserole

The first threshing machine—built by John and Hiram Pitts of Winthrop, Maine, in 1834—harvested grains, beans, and seed crops more efficiently than hand methods, and threshing became an honorable occupation. This institution is preserved by the Midwest Old Threshers, centered in southeast Iowa at Mount Pleasant. They endorse this recipe, originally reprinted in an old farm journal.

Stewing chickens 2, 4 pounds
Water
Salt 1 teaspoon
Celery 2 stalks, chopped
Medium onion 1, chopped
Whole wheat bread 6 cups torn in ½-inch pieces
Salt ¾ teaspoon
Pepper dash
Onion 2 tablespoons finely chopped
Sage dash (optional)
Flour 4 tablespoons

Put chicken in a large kettle, cover with water, and add salt, celery, and onion. Cook on low heat part of stove about 2 to 3 hours until chicken is tender. Remove chicken, cool, and cube. Strain broth, cool, and remove fat. You may do this a day ahead. The next day, put chicken in large greased 2-quart casserole or Dutch oven. Mix together next 4 ingredients, and sage if desired. Lay over chicken. Stir flour into 1 quart of broth. Pour over chicken and dressing. Cover tightly, place on trivet on stove top, and let cook about 2 to 3 hours until casserole is bound together. Serves 8.
Note: On a conventional range, cook at 350° for 35 minutes.

Mission Chicken

Spanish Catholic priests spearheaded the planting of vineyards and orchards in southern California as they set up missions to feed the bodies and souls of natives and settlers. In an old cast-iron kettle on the back of the mission kitchen stove, this chicken simmered to be glorified on the platter by the bounty of California's vineyards and orchards.

Butter 2 tablespoons
Chicken fryer 1, 2½ pounds, cut up
Cinnamon ¼ teaspoon
Cloves ¼ teaspoon

Salt 1 teaspoon
Fresh orange juice 1 cup
Madeira wine ½ cup
Hot pepper sauce 2 or 3 drops
Seedless grapes 1 cup halved
Flour 1 tablespoon
Slivered almonds ½ cup, toasted
Orange 1, sliced

Melt butter in 2-quart kettle and brown chicken. Combine next 6 ingredients and pour over chicken. Tightly cover kettle and cook slowly on low heat part of stove about 4 or 5 hours until chicken is tender. Remove chicken from kettle and arrange on a platter. Put grapes over chicken. Thicken sauce remaining in kettle with flour. Spoon over chicken and sprinkle with toasted almonds. Garnish with orange slices. Serves 4 to 6.

Chicken Fricassee

As a society belle, Martha Washington had more on her mind than kitchen arts and cookery. When she married her first husband, Daniel Parke Custis, her mother-in-law kindly wrote by hand some two hundred "receipts" in a Booke of Cookery, *which included instructions for "frykacie" of chicken.*

Chicken 1, 3 pounds, cut up
Flour 2 tablespoons
Butter 2 tablespoons
Water 2 cups
Small white onions 12
Thyme pinch
Celery salt pinch
Sage pinch
Egg yolk 1, beaten
Rice 4 cups cooked

Roll chicken in flour and brown in butter. Add water, onions, and seasonings. Cover and place pan on trivet on stove top. Cook about an hour until chicken is tender, adding water during cooking to keep chicken covered with liquid. At end of cooking time, remove 3 tablespoons of hot liquid from the pot and stir into egg yolk. Stir thoroughly, return to pot, and cook about 10 more minutes. Serve over rice. Serves 6.

Country Captain

Legend says this spiced chicken was introduced into Savannah, Georgia, by a ship's captain who engaged in the spice trade. The name of this recipe may well be a tribute to the die-hard ship captain who brought precious spices to the kitchen hearth.

Chicken fryer   1, 3 pounds, cut up
Salt and pepper   to taste
Butter   3 tablespoons, melted
Onion   ½ cup minced
Green pepper   1, diced
Celery   1 cup diced
Garlic clove   1, minced
Curry powder   2 teaspoons
Thyme   ½ teaspoon crushed
Tomatoes   28-ounce can, coarsely chopped
Salt   1 teaspoon
Currants   ¼ cup (optional)
Sliced almonds   ¼ cup toasted
Parsley   2 tablespoons

Pat chicken dry and sprinkle with salt and pepper. Melt butter in skillet on stove top. Brown chicken on both sides, then place chicken in a 2-quart casserole dish. Add next 4 ingredients to butter and cook until soft. Stir in curry powder, then thyme, and cook briefly. Add tomatoes with liquid and salt. Stir and pour over chicken. Cover casserole, set on a trivet on stove top, and let simmer about 1½ hours until chicken is done. Turn chicken over in sauce. Garnish with currants, almonds, and parsley. Serves 4.

Chicken and Mushrooms

In A Portland Girl's Chafing Dish Cookbook *of 1897, Alice H. Sansbury advocated women's liberation from kitchen slavery. Even though the cook had to work ahead to simmer the chicken and gather everything she needed on a tray, she refused to hide in her kitchen when her guests came. She put everything together at the last minute and heated a pot on a rack over a flame. Wood stove tops function as well as a chafing dish for liberating a woman from the kitchen. Start with this dish from the Portland girl.*

Chicken   1, 3 pounds
Celery   1 stalk, chopped
Small onion   ½, sliced
Peppercorns   3
Carrot   1, sliced
Water
Butter   ½ cup
Cornstarch   2 teaspoons
Cream   ¾ cup
Egg yolks   3
Salt
Butter
Mushrooms   1 cup sliced
Paprika   garnish
Wild rice   cooked

Wash chicken and put it in pot with next 5 ingredients. Simmer about 2 or 3 hours. Cool, bone meat, and cut into large pieces. Strain stock, cool, then skim fat. Assemble chicken and other ingredients on a tray. Just before serving, heat heavy pot on stove top. Melt ½ cup butter, stir in cornstarch, add stock, and simmer until slightly thickened. Mix cream and egg yolks together and add slowly to stock mixture. Add chicken and salt. Meanwhile, melt butter in small pan and sauté mushrooms. Add mushrooms to chicken mixture, then heat through but do not boil. Sprinkle with paprika and serve with rice. Serves 4 to 6.

Chicken and Dumplings

Men were pulled from American homes into foreign foxholes when the Germans marched into Poland on 1 September 1939. Women left alone during World War II managed on scant incomes and rationed foods, and some raised Rhode Island reds in their backyards for eggs and meat. One young Oregon girl remembers the day the war ended—2 September 1945. She was in downtown Portland, amid flying confetti and bumper-to-bumper traffic, while still dressed in clothes spattered with blood from chickens she and her mother had been killing for the stewpot.

Chicken   1, 3 pounds
Boiling water   2 quarts
Salt   ½ teaspoon
Pepper   ¼ teaspoon
Butter   ¼ cup
Flour   ¼ cup
Milk   2 cups
Dumplings

Cut chicken in pieces and put in water in heavy 5-quart pot. Cook on back of stove about 2 hours until tender. Remove chicken from broth. Strain and reserve broth. Season chicken with salt and pepper. In large kettle melt butter and add flour. Cook until frothy, then stir in broth reserved from chicken and milk and cook until sauce thickens. Return chicken to sauce and bring to simmer. Drop in spoonfuls of dumpling batter and simmer covered about 20 minutes. Serves 6 to 8.

Dumplings

Flour   2 cups
Baking powder   1½ teaspoons
Salt   ½ teaspoon
Egg   1
Milk   about 1 cup

Mix flour with baking powder and salt. Beat egg in a cup and fill with milk. Stir into flour mixture.

Paella

Spain ruled Mexico, then Mexico ruled California until an angry band of American settlers staged the Bear Flag Revolt in June 1846. They captured Mexican headquarters and unfurled a patchwork star and bear proclaiming the "California Republic." Two years later the United States won the war and rejected Mexico, but not this elegant Spanish dish of the territory.

Chicken breasts*   2
Water   6 cups
Olive oil   1 cup
Brown rice   2 cups uncooked
Ham*   ¾ cup cooked and diced
Onion   1, chopped
Shrimp*   6, shelled and deveined
Clams*   12, shelled and washed
Peas   ½ cup cooked
Bell pepper   1, diced
Green olives   12, pitted
Salt and pepper   to taste

Boil chicken in water about 30 to 60 minutes until done. Heat oil in skillet on stove top. Add rice, ham, and onion. Stir until rice is coated with oil. Add chicken and broth, and all remaining ingredients. Bring to simmer, cover, and cook about 30 minutes or until rice absorbs liquid. Serve 6 to 8.
* Or use whatever other meat and seafood you have available.
Note: In a conventional oven, cook at 350° for 45 minutes.

Wickford Quahog Pie

When clergyman Roger Williams was run out of Massachusetts Bay Colony for his "absurd" belief that the king of England should pay New World Indians for the land he granted, he took refuge in Rhode Island, paid the Indians for it, and lived off the waters' bounty. Although Rhode Island is the smallest state in the country, its forty-mile coastline and thirteen rivers make it one of the richest areas of marine life on the East Coast. This clam pie, named for a Rhode Island town and the state's famous clams, comes from the state's early days.

Quahogs* 1 pint, chopped
Flour 1 tablespoon
Butter 2 tablespoons
Water 1 cup
Pepper dash
Tabasco sauce dash
Biscuit dough

Combine all ingredients except dough and put in a deep 1½-quart casserole. Roll out dough until it is ½-inch thick and the diameter of the casserole. Put dough on top of clams. Set casserole on a trivet on the stove top, cover tightly, and cook until dough is set and sauce is thick. Serves 4 to 6.

* Clams that thrive in Rhode Island waters. Any kind of clam (6½-ounce can, chopped) may be substituted.
Note: In a conventional oven, cook at 375° for 20 minutes.

Biscuit Dough

Flour 2 cups sifted
Baking powder 2½ teaspoons
Salt 1 teaspoon
Butter ⅓ cup
Milk ⅔ cup

Combine flour, baking powder, and salt in mixing bowl. Blend in butter with pastry blender or 2 knives until mixture turns into fine particles. Add milk and stir with fork until dough holds together. Gather into ball and knead gently on lightly floured board.

"Too Stew Oystors"

English Quaker William Penn founded "Penn's Woods" or Pennsylvania as a sanctuary for Quakers to escape scorn, ridicule, and imprisonment in 1680. When Penn asked King Charles II to repay a debt to his late father in American wilderness land, Charles consented and gave Penn complete rule of this piece of New World territory. As a proper Quaker, Penn observed neither feasting nor fasting. But his account books record purchase of "oystors" by the barrel. This recipe from the household records of his first wife, who never came to America, was tucked in her son's satchel when he visited Pennsbury Manor in 1703. At the end of the recipe she suggests, "So send them up with sipets of frentch breed . . ."

Oysters 1 quart, plus juice
Small onion 1, sliced
Mace ⅛ teaspoon
Peppercorns ¼ teaspoon
White wine 2 cups
Anchovies 4 (optional)
Butter 1 cup
Lemon juice of 1 lemon

Put oysters in a skillet with their juice, onion, mace, and peppercorns. Put on stove top and simmer until liquid is almost gone and onions are limp. Remove oysters and put in another pan. Add wine to oysters and simmer about 30 minutes. Add anchovies, if desired, and simmer until liquid is thick. Add butter and lemon juice. Serves 6 to 8.

Hangtown Fry

A carpenter building a sawmill on a California river chanced to see shimmering bits of gold in the mill race. Rumors of his discovery flew to the East Coast but were mired in the financial depression caused by the Mexican War effort of 1846. The California governor felt obliged to notify the war department that there was sufficient gold in one small region of California to pay for the war a hundred times over. The 1849 gold rush was on. Some 75,000 treasure seekers poured into the area around San Francisco to mine $81 million of gold in 1852 alone. Lucky miners paid outlandish food prices in sacks of gold. One hungry miner staggered into a hotel, threw down a handful of gold nuggets, and demanded the most expensive meal the cook could prepare. Since eggs sold for a dollar a piece, this is what he got.

Oysters 6
Flour ¼ cup
Salt and pepper to taste
Eggs 5
Fine cracker crumbs
Butter 1½ tablespoons

Drain oysters and dip in flour seasoned with salt and pepper. Then dip in 1 well-beaten egg and then in cracker crumbs. Heat butter in skillet and fry oysters until brown on both sides. Beat remaining eggs with salt and pepper. Pour over oysters and cook until eggs are set. Turn over in skillet and briefly cook other side. Serves 4 (or 1 famished miner).

Maryland Crab Cakes

John Smith, soldier, adventurer, and a member of the first English colony in America—Jamestown 1607—was fearless! After engineering the building of defenses against hostile Indians and securing corn for the first winter from friendly Indians, he piled fourteen men into an open boat and explored the Chesapeake Bay inch by inch. He produced a map fine enough to define the boundaries of the colonies in later days. For his excursion around the bay, he packed "nothing but a little meale...and water..." and counted on "...fish as we caught by accident." When the men failed to catch fish with a frying pan, they resorted to their spears. Captain Smith accidently speared a stingray and was so badly injured that he ordered his men to say his funeral and dig his grave. He recovered in time to eat fish for supper, however. He may have eaten crab, so plentiful in the Chesapeake Bay. Settlers who followed Smith perfected this Maryland Crab Cake, famous even today in Baltimore.

Crab meat 6½-ounce can or
    Fresh crab ½ pound
Crackers 6, unsalted, crushed
Egg 1, beaten
Parsley ¼ cup chopped
Worchestershire sauce 1½ teaspoons
Hot mustard ½ teaspoon
Mayonnaise 2 teaspoons
Salt and pepper to taste
Butter 2 tablespoons
Saltines
Mustard

Mix together crab meat, crackers, egg, parsley, Worchestershire sauce, hot mustard, mayonnaise, salt, and pepper. Form into cakes. Melt butter in cast-iron skillet. Place cakes in skillet and cook on one side. Turn to cook on second side. Serve with saltines and mustard. Serves 4.

Salmon in Ashes

"The salmon they are playing, and leapin' in the brook, Sir. They hop into your kettle, put the cover on, and cook, Sir." Despite this nineteenth-century enticement that was sent to Europe from our land of plenty, you know how precious is the salmon in today's kettle. Cook it with finesse just before stove-cleaning time when ashes are plentiful enough to insulate the fish.

Salt to taste
Lemon juice to taste
Salmon* 1, 3 pounds, cleaned
Parsley 2 tablespoons
Fresh tarragon 3 crushed leaves or
    Dried tarragon ½ teaspoon
Salt ¼ teaspoon
Pepper ⅛ teaspoon
Bacon 4 or 5 strips

Rub salt and lemon juice over fish. Mix together next 4 ingredients and lightly rub inside of fish. Wrap fish several times with bacon, then wrap securely in heavy foil. Bury in hot ashes away from red coals or flaming logs in outer edges of firebox. Bake about 7 minutes for every inch of thickness of the fish, turning halfway through baking. Serves 4 to 6.
* You can use any whole fish.

126   Main Dishes

Poached Salmon

Salmon were so abundant in the Pacific Northwest waters of yesteryear that the earliest English, French, and Spanish adventurers who came to the region had no worries about food. Later emigrant settlers who reached the end of the Oregon Trail in the fall of the year could survive their first winter because of this rich fish. Its delicate pink flesh is still savored, especially when cooked this way.

Water   3 quarts
Dry white wine   2 cups
Carrots   2, sliced
Celery   2 stalks, with leaves
Large onion   1, sliced
Parsley   3 sprigs
Thyme   ¼ teaspoon
Peppercorns   5
Salt   1 tablespoon
Salmon*   1, 3 pounds, cleaned
Lemon slices   garnish
Parsley   sprigs, garnish

Simmer all ingredients except fish and garnishes for 10 minutes in fish poacher. Add fish and simmer 10 minutes for every inch of thickness of the fish. Lift gently from poacher and put on platter. Garnish with lemon and parsley. Serves 4 to 6.
* Or use any whole fish.
Note: Save liquid for later use. You may want to reduce it by simmering it longer and using it for fish stock. It keeps up to 2 days in refrigerator and freezes well.

Norwegian Salmon Pudding

Norway's population doubled in the late 1800s when sanitation and medical treatment improved and the cultivation of potatoes spread. Overcrowded Norwegians overflowed from their homeland into America, attracted by the Pacific Northwest halibut, salmon, and whaling ship areas, as well as the open western lands. Today in the Puget Sound, descendants of these Norwegians catch salmon at night with gill nets. Wives sometimes "crew" for their husbands and cook their catch this old Norwegian way.

Salmon 1½ pounds, cleaned
Salt 2 teaspoons
Nutmeg ¼ teaspoon
Butter or margarine ¼ cup, melted
Milk 2 cups

Remove skin and bones from salmon and blend in a bowl with salt and nutmeg. Beat with an electric mixer 10 minutes, gradually adding butter while you beat. Add milk gradually and continue beating. Beat 15 more minutes after adding milk. (Shorten beating time by processing ingredients in this same order in a blender.) Pour into greased 1½-quart baking dish. Place dish on rack inside kettle filled with 1 inch of water. Cover kettle and set on stove top to cook about 1½ to 2 hours until pudding tests done when a knife is inserted in the center. Serves 6.

Brook Trout with Chablis and Dill

In the early days of our country, trout were so plentiful that a fisherman could make a catch with a bare hook. But as fish became fewer, they became smarter and wiser to the waders in their waters. Then fishermen had to camouflage their hooks with bits of silk and wool, feather and fur to resemble flies and insects, the fish's natural diet. From the creel of a sport fisherman comes this recipe.

Trout 4 to 6, each weighing about 1 pound
Butter ¼ cup, melted
Thin lemon slices of 1 lemon
Salt and pepper to taste
Fresh dill 1 tablespoon chopped or
    Dried dill ½ teaspoon
Lemon juice of 1 lemon
Butter ½ cup
Heavy cream 1 cup
Chablis wine ¾ cup

Clean fish and place in a greased 9 by 13-inch baking pan. Pour butter over fish. Cover fish with lemon and sprinkle with salt, pepper, and dill. Cover pan tightly with foil and place on trivet on stove top. Let cook about 20 minutes until fish is flaky. In a saucepan, combine lemon juice, butter, and cream. Slowly add wine. When fish is done and sauce ingredients are blended, pour over fish in baking pan and serve. Serves 4 to 6.

128   Main Dishes

Baked Trout with Sour Cream

Fishermen are rich or poor, male or female, child or adult, famous or ordinary folk who escape their worries and chores with the benefit of a fish in the dinner pan. Many United States presidents—Grover Cleveland, Herbert Hoover, Franklin D. Roosevelt, Dwight D. Eisenhower—have taken our country's problems and a fishing pole to fish-filled lakes and streams and renewed their visions and vigor from the relaxing escape. Bake this trout over a camp stove as did the fisherman who originated it, or cook it on the stove top. Be prepared to miss the mosquitoes and the sunset.

Trout   1, cleaned
Salt and pepper   to taste
Worcestershire sauce   1 teaspoon
Prepared mustard   1 teaspoon
Lemon juice   3 tablespoons
Sour cream   1½ cups
Onions   1 cup, chopped

Clean trout, then place in greased casserole dish or baking pan that fits the fish. Salt and pepper trout. Mix remaining ingredients and fill fish with the sauce. Pour remaining sauce over fish. Cover, place pan on trivet, and bake about an hour until fish flakes. Serves 4.
Note: In a conventional oven, bake at 350° for 1 hour.

Pine-Bark Fish Stew

Cooked long and slow so it would thicken, this stew was served to South Carolina farmhands on a piece of pine bark—forerunner of the paper plate.

Bacon   6 strips
Medium onions   6, quartered and sliced
Water   2 cups
Butter or margarine   3 tablespoons
Fish   3 pounds, cut into serving-sized pieces
Salt   to taste
Black pepper   ⅛ teaspoon
Red pepper   ⅛ teaspoon
Worcestershire sauce   1 teaspoon
Canned tomatoes   28-ounce can
Tomato sauce   6-ounce can
Rice   4 cups cooked

Cook bacon until crisp and remove from pan. Slowly fry onions in bacon grease. Add water and butter and simmer until blended. Drop in fish and add remaining ingredients except bacon and rice. Simmer slowly until fish is tender. Break bacon into small pieces and drop into stew. Serve on rice. Serves 6 to 8.

Filbert Pie

Declaring that filberts would not grow commercially in the United States, botanists were ready to toss in their nutcrackers fifty years ago. Europeans would have to grow this finicky nut that requires winter pollination by wind, rich, well-drained soil, and mild weather—perfect growing conditions. But to their surprise, botanists discovered the fifty trees that Frenchman David Garnot had planted along a fencerow in Oregon's Willamette Valley. Today 95 percent of the commercial filbert crop is grown in the Willamette Valley. Named for St. Philbert, whose feast day comes in August when the nut ripens, the filbert is indeed a special nut.

Broccoli 1 cup chopped and steamed
Cauliflower 1 cup sliced and steamed
Spinach 1 cup chopped
Onion ¼ cup diced
Green pepper ½ cup diced
Cheddar cheese 1 cup grated
Filberts (Hazelnuts) 1 cup coarsely chopped
Salt ½ teaspoon
Whole wheat flour ¼ cup
Unbleached white flour ¾ cup
Baking powder 2 teaspoons
Milk 1½ cups
Eggs 4
Garlic 1 clove, pressed
Pepper ¼ teaspoon

Mix together broccoli, cauliflower, spinach, onion, green pepper, and cheese in a deep, well-greased 10-inch baking dish. Top with filberts. In a bowl, blend salt, flours, and baking powder. Beat in milk, eggs, garlic, and pepper. Pour mixture over vegetables and nuts. Set baking dish on trivet and place on stove top. Cover with larger, inverted pan. Cook about 1 hour until pie is set, and blade of knife comes out clean. Serves 6 to 8.
Note: In a conventional oven, bake at 400° for 35 to 40 minutes.

Cheese Fondue

Emily Post (1873–1960), our matron of manners until she died, told our upwardly mobile society that if we used common sense and regarded other people's feelings, we would weather any social situation. She also groomed our table manners. Our American ancestors had rejected English formalities and had even eaten with knives from a communal pot. Although our modern table manners usually are quite sophisticated, you can return to dipping again from a communal pot on the wood stove with this fondue.

Garlic clove 1
Gruyère cheese ½ pound, shredded
Swiss cheese ½ pound, shredded
Flour 3 tablespoons
Dry white wine 2 cups
Lemon juice 1 tablespoon
Nutmeg dash
Salt ⅛ teaspoon
Pepper dash
French or Italian bread 3 cups cubed
Turkey or chicken 2 cups cooked and cubed
Shrimp 1 cup cooked, shelled, and deveined
Vegetables 3 cups raw or cooked

Rub inside of heavy pot with garlic and discard clove. Toss cheese with flour. Pour wine into pot and set over low heat part of stove. When small bubbles appear on bottom, stir in lemon juice and cheese. Stir until cheese melts. Stir in nutmeg, salt, and pepper. Serve with bread, meat, and/or vegetables. Serves 4 to 6.

Welsh Rabbit

The truth may never be known about Welsh rarebit, or is it rabbit? Is it really a Welsh dish or is it an English poke at Wales? Whatever the answers, the dish has been made in the United States for perhaps as long as white men and cows have been here. It uses Cheddar cheese, first made in America by a factory in Herkimer, New York, in the mid-1800s. Use beer in this recipe for the Early American version.

Butter   1 tablespoon
Sharp Cheddar cheese   1 pound, grated
Beer or heavy cream   ¾ cup
Cayenne   dash
Dry mustard   1 teaspoon
Salt   ½ teaspoon
Worcestershire sauce   ½ teaspoon
Egg   1, slightly beaten
Toast points or crackers   (optional)

Melt butter in saucepan. Add cheese and all except 1 tablespoon beer. Cook until cheese melts. Combine seasonings with remaining liquid and stir slowly into cheese mixture. Stir in egg. Serve on toast points or use as cold spread. Serves 4 to 6.

Cheese-Herb Frittata

Italians cringe at Americans' conception of their national cuisine—pizza and tomato sauces. Since the tomato was not even used as a food in Europe until 1830, the Italians had time to develop such exciting dishes as this "peasant omelet" before over five million Italians came to settle from California's wine-growing regions to New York City.

Butter   3 tablespoons
Green onion   1, thinly sliced
Parsley   1 tablespoon chopped
Eggs   8
Sour cream   ½ cup
Fresh basil   2 tablespoons chopped or
　　Dried basil   ½ teaspoon
Salt   ½ teaspoon
Pepper   to taste
Parmesan cheese   ⅓ cup grated

Melt butter in skillet over hot spot of stove. Add onion and parsley and cook until onion wilts. Beat eggs with wire whip and gradually add sour cream. Continue beating a few minutes, then add basil, salt, and pepper. Pour egg mixture over butter and onion and cook to set, lifting sides of egg to allow all to cook. Sprinkle cheese over eggs, cover, and cook until cheese melts. Serves 4 to 6.

Corn Oysters

The ideal eastern farm of the mid-1700s was carved out of dense virgin forest. A zigzag split-rail fence kept the Dorset Horn sheep, Chincoteague ponies, and pigs out of the garden. The main cabin, a tobacco barn, and a smoke house were separated by a kitchen garden; an herb garden for medicine, cosmetics, and culinary flavorings; a grape arbor for wine; and the fields of wheat, vegetables, and corn. Corn grew profusely, especially in Maryland where they ate these corn oysters (corn fritters)—a mainstay when meat and fish were scarce.

Corn 10-ounce package
Egg 1, beaten
Butter 2 tablespoons, melted
Buttermilk ⅔ cup
Salt ¼ teaspoon
Pepper to taste
Flour ⅔ cup
Oil for frying
Maple syrup

Combine first 6 ingredients in bowl. Mix together well and stir in flour until smooth. Put oil in iron skillet on stove top. When oil is sizzling hot, drop in corn mixture a teaspoonful at a time. Turn fritters to brown on other side. Serve with maple syrup. Makes 36.

Cornmeal Mush

The Hawn family of Eugene Township, Indiana, has been eating this fried corn dish for several generations. That town, perched on the banks of the Vermillion River, sits crooked with the world. The streets run SE¼ and NW¼, not SE and NW. When the surveyor Stephen S. Collett laid out the town from the front door of the water-powered gristmill in 1827, his compass was off by three degrees and twenty-five minutes. But the Hawns and other families moved straight into the day after eating the fried cornmeal mush that had cooked on the banked stove all night.

Cornmeal 1 cup
Cold water 1 cup
Salt 1 teaspoon
Boiling water 2¾ cups
Flour
Butter
Maple syrup

The night before, combine cornmeal, cold water, and salt in a heavy 2-quart saucepan or iron pot. Stir in boiling water. Continue stirring and bring to boil. Place on trivet and let sit until water is absorbed or overnight. Pour into greased 9 by 5 by 3-inch loaf pan to cool. Remove from pan and cut into ½-inch slices. Dredge in flour and slowly brown in butter melted in iron skillet on stove top. Serve hot with butter and maple syrup. Serves 4.

Barley-Mushroom Casserole

A communal movement swept from the West Coast to the East Coast in the late 1960s and early 1970s. One could travel across the country staying at a counter-cultural community every night. Most groups were agrarian, but some thrived in the heart of New York City. Among other things, they shared a commitment to vegetarianism. Many communitarians have drifted back into "straight" society, with their knowledge of wood stoves and simplified living. This recipe is typical of the commune diet.

Butter　6 tablespoons
Onions　2, chopped
Garlic cloves　2, minced
Barley　1 cup
Water or Vegetable Stock (see Index)　1⅓ cups
Mushrooms　1 cup sliced
Salt and pepper　to taste
Parsley　2 tablespoons chopped
Dried thyme　1 teaspoon
Dried sage　1 teaspoon
Dried rosemary　1 teaspoon

Melt butter in small pan over hot spot of stove. Sauté onions and garlic. Stir in barley and continue cooking about 10 minutes, then combine these ingredients in Dutch oven with remaining ingredients. Cover, place on trivet, and simmer on stove top about 1 to 2 hours until liquid is absorbed, tastes are blended, and texture is tender. Serves 6.

Russian Mushrooms

Russian fur traders charted a course across the Bering Sea into Alaska as early as 1747. Settlers, traders, and missionaries later followed, then gradually filtered down the Pacific coast. When Alaska was sold to the United States after the Civil War, many of them returned home. One food we can identify with our Russian ancestors is the mushroom. When dried, it traveled well in the pioneers' haversacks. In this old recipe, mushrooms are combined with two other truly Russian ingredients—cabbage and sour cream. Simmered overnight atop the stove, it is a real Russian breakfast treat.

Large dried mushrooms   6
Water   6 cups
Red cabbage   2 pounds, shredded
Salt   to taste
Sour cream   1 cup
Butter   1 tablespoon
Flour   1 tablespoon

Put mushrooms in water and stew them until soft. Parboil cabbage separately about 15 minutes, then drain. Drain broth off mushrooms and pour broth over cabbage. Mince mushrooms and add to cabbage, then add salt. Simmer cabbage and mushrooms until liquid is absorbed, then pour sour cream over the mixture. In saucepan, melt butter, then brown flour. Pour butter and flour into cabbage and mushrooms. Cover and simmer slowly about an hour until liquid is cooked down and cabbage is tender. Serves 6.

Breads and Such

" . . . Bread to a man with a hungry family comes first," said John L. Lewis, "before his union, before his citizenship, before his church affiliation. Bread!"

And so essential is bread that it generated "American ingenuity" as soon as the Pilgrims stepped off the boat and learned that wheat grew poorly in New England soil. They substituted Indian meal, oats, and rye that did grow easily and added the luxury of leavening from beer, sourdough, soda, and sour milk. Or as General Custer's cook did on the western plains of war, they made baking powder of cream of tartar (two tablespoons), baking soda (one tablespoon), and cornstarch (one tablespoon).

Boston Brown Bread

Both Indians and colonists ate the rustic ryaninjun *bread made of ground corn and rye flour. Boston brown bread evolved from that bread. Puritans of seventeenth-century Boston served it with their beans on Sunday because "Brown Bread and the Gospel are good fare."*

Rye flour 1 cup
Cornmeal 1 cup
Whole wheat flour 1 cup
Baking soda 1 tablespoon
Salt 1 teaspoon
Raisins 1 cup
Molasses ¾ cup
Buttermilk 2 cups

Mix dry ingredients together, reserving 3 tablespoons wheat flour to coat raisins. Stir in coated raisins, molasses, and buttermilk, and blend well. Pour into 2 greased 1-pound coffee cans, cover with foil, and tie with string. Set on rack in kettle of simmering water that comes halfway up side of can. Cover kettle and steam about 3 hours until broom straw comes out clean. Makes 2 loaves.

War Brown Bread

Town leaders of Elizabethtown, New Jersey, were on the verge of accepting Britain's offer of amnesty in December of 1776. But Hannah Arnett, whose home they were meeting in, threatened to leave her husband if he should forsake the cause. She implied that all the men were traitors for considering acceptance. Hearing that story, a group of women descendants of Revolutionary War soldiers formed the Daughters of the American Revolution. *America's fan club has taken on many causes to show its "noble and holy patriotism." One president, Mrs. Matthew T. Scott, encouraged home economics as a means of patriotism, and this recipe, developed by one chapter of the* DAR *in 1917, proved her point by freeing up foodstuffs for the Allies.*

Yellow cornmeal 2 cups
Graham flour 2 cups
Baking powder 2 teaspoons
Baking soda 2 teaspoons
Salt 2 teaspoons
Shortening 3 tablespoons
Sour milk 3 cups
Molasses ¾ cup
Sugar ¼ cup

Mix all ingredients together, adding one at a time. Pour into 2 greased 5 by 9-inch bread pans. Place pans on trivets on stove top and cover with inverted roasting pan. Bake 1½ to 2 hours until broom straw comes out clean.
Note: In a conventional oven, bake at 250° for 1½ to 2 hours.

Oat Bread

Oats planted in the Elizabeth Isles off the coast of Massachusetts in 1602 by a sea captain flourished and the colonists gratefully harvested and processed them for breakfast. By 1854 a housewife could buy them, packaged in glass jars, at the general store. In 1912 she could pick them off the shelf herself in the first self-service grocery store—Alpha Beta Food Market in Pomona, California. Today she throws a cylindrical box with a smiling man in a blue hat into her wire pushcart as she scurries down the aisle of the all-American institution—a supermarket.

Whole wheat flour 2 cups
Rolled oats 1 cup
Unprocessed bran 1 cup
Brown sugar 1 cup packed
Baking soda 1½ teaspoons
Lemon zest 1 teaspoon
Eggs 2
Buttermilk 1½ cups
Vegetable oil ¼ cup
Prunes 2 cups reconstituted and chopped

Stir all ingredients together in a mixing bowl. Pour batter into a greased 9 by 5-inch loaf pan and put on trivet on stove top. Cover with larger pan and bake 1 hour or longer, checking for doneness with a broom straw. Remove from heat and cool 10 minutes, then turn onto rack and cool. Makes 1 loaf.

Kansas Corn Cake

Congress gave settlers in Kansas the right to decide whether they wanted slavery when they passed the Kansas-Nebraska Act of 1854. Bloodshed that followed earned Kansans one of their many nicknames—Jayhawkers (antislavery fighters). John J. Ingalls, a literary senator, wrote the first official state motto, which reflects those turbulent times—Ad astra per aspera or "To the Stars Through Difficulties." This breakfast bread is from his wife's cookbook.

Indian meal*   2 cups
Sugar   1 cup
Flour   2 cups sifted
Baking powder   3 heaping teaspoons
Butter   ½ cup
Eggs   2
Milk   2 cups

Combine first 4 ingredients. Melt butter in baking tin on stove top. Beat together eggs and milk and pour in butter. Combine dry ingredients with liquid and beat well. Pour into two 8-inch square cake pans. Place on trivet on stove top and cover with larger pan. Cook about 20 to 30 minutes until broom straw comes out clean. Serves 6 to 8.
* Coarse yellow cornmeal.
Note: In a conventional oven, bake at 350° for 20 minutes.

Corn Bread

Corn, more than any other food, prevented starvation in early America. Europeans first heard of corn when they came to this country, and the Indians taught them how to grow, dry, and grind it. The dried meal was mixed with salt and water and cooked as mush, bread, or cake. Through the years corn bread has had many textures—hard, soft, moist, or dry—and many shapes—as ash cakes, corn sticks, hoecakes, corn pone, or just plain corn bread. To southerners it still remains "Our Daily Bread." This is the favorite corn bread recipe of Mrs. Tecolia Leola Deborah Warner, known as Pecolia for short. She is a seventy-eight-year-old quilt maker from Yazoo City, Mississippi.

White cornmeal   2 scant cups
Flour   ½ cup
Baking powder   1½ teaspoons
Salt   ½ teaspoon
Sugar   ½ teaspoon
Milk or evaporated milk   ½ cup
Water   ½ cup
Shortening   1 tablespoon melted
Egg   1

Sift together first 5 ingredients, then stir in milk and water. Add shortening and egg and mix well. Heat baking pan by sitting it on stove top. Melt shortening in it and tip around to coat inside of pan. Pour in corn bread mixture. Sit on trivet on stove top and cover with larger pan. Cook until broom straw comes out clean.
Note: In a conventional oven, bake at 325° for 25 to 30 minutes.

Mennonite Corn Bread

Old Order Mennonite corn bread is moist and heavy. After serving it hot for supper, eat it in a bowl with milk for breakfast the next morning.

Coarse yellow cornmeal   1 cup
Flour   1 cup
Baking powder   2 teaspoons
Baking soda   1½ teaspoons
Brown sugar   3 tablespoons
Salt   1 teaspoon
Eggs   2
Buttermilk   1½ cups
Butter or margarine   3 tablespoons, melted
Vanilla   2 teaspoons

Mix dry ingredients. Add remaining ingredients and beat together well. Pour into two greased 8-inch round cake pans. Place on trivet on stove top and cover with larger baking pan or roasting pan. Bake 20 to 30 minutes until it tests done with a broom straw or knife. Serves 8 to 10.
Note: In a conventional oven, bake at 450° for 20 minutes.

Smoky Mountain Corn Bread

This is one of some twenty recipes for corn bread listed in a cookbook from the "Great Smokie Mountains of Tennessee." In that region, isolated settlers were completely self-sufficient with cornmeal, molasses, and honey all from their cornfield, sorghum patch, and bee "gums." Somewhere along the creek in a settled mountain hollow was sure to be a small mill for grinding the corn into meal.

Sugar ½ cup
Salt ½ teaspoon
Cornmeal 1 cup
Flour 1 cup
Baking soda 1 teaspoon
Baking powder 2 teaspoons
Eggs 2
Shortening 2 tablespoons, melted
Milk 1 cup

Mix dry ingredients together. Stir in remaining ingredients, then pour into a greased 8-inch square pan. Place on trivet on stove top and cover with larger pan. Bake about 30 minutes until broom straw comes out clean. Serves 6.
Note: In a conventional oven, bake at 350° for 25 to 30 minutes.

Ash Cakes

Ash cakes are an "instant" corn bread. They cook right in the ashes. A traveler would simply throw a hunk of dough into his campfire to cook. But at home, cooks with more delicate palates could achieve a more delicate flavor by wrapping the cakes in cabbage leaves before putting them in the ashes.

Cornmeal 2 cups
Baking soda ¾ teaspoon
Salt 1 teaspoon
Buttermilk 1 cup
Shortening ⅓ cup, melted
Water

Combine cornmeal, soda, and salt. Combine buttermilk and shortening. Mix dry ingredients with liquid. Add enough water to make stiff dough, then form into patties. Get a good hot fire going. Open the stove door (if this can be done without smoking up the house). Pull ashes into a pile and make a nestlike place in the firebox. Put dough in the nest. Cover to insulate with ashes and place hot embers over the cakes. Bake about 20 to 30 minutes until dough is set. Remove from ashes. Drop into pan of water and remove quickly to set and dry by their own heat. (Wrap dough in greased foil or cabbage leaves, if desired.) Serves 6.

"Pot Likker" Corn Bread

"Kingfish" was a powerful Louisiana politician named Huey P. Long (1893-1935). He started a program that gave free textbooks to schoolchildren, instigated another that built a massive highway and bridge system throughout his state, and dictated many social reforms before an assassin stopped him. His definition of "Pot Likker" appears in the United States Congressional Record: "the residue that remains from the commingling, heating and evaporation—anyway, it is in the bottom of the pot when greens are cooked." This one-hundred-year-old recipe from Tennessee cooks the corn bread like dumplings right in the "pot likker."

Turnip greens 2 or 3 bunches
Water
Ham hock 1
Green onion 2 tablespoons finely minced
Cornmeal 1½ cups
Salt ½ teaspoon
Black pepper ¼ teaspoon
Egg 1

Put greens in large pot and cover with water. Add ham and simmer on stove top for several hours until all are tender. Mix onion into cornmeal. Season with salt and pepper. Stir in enough liquid from the greens to make a stiff dough. When mixture has cooled slightly, mix in egg. Shape into small patties about ½-inch thick. Lay gently on top of simmering greens. Cover and simmer about 10 to 15 minutes until dough appears firm. Serves 4.

Spoon Bread

Spoon bread is the queen of corn breads. It is served on elegant occasions in the finest of restaurants and in homes throughout the South as a meat accompaniment and is truly served with a spoon.

Cornmeal   ¾ cup
Salt   1 teaspoon
Sugar   1 tablespoon
Butter   2 tablespoons
Water   1 cup
Milk   2 cups
Eggs   3, well beaten
Butter

Combine first 5 ingredients and 1 cup milk in saucepan. Place on stove top and stir until mixture thickens. Remove from heat and cool. Beat remaining milk and eggs together, stir into cornmeal mixture, and pour into a greased, heavy, 1½-quart baking dish. Set on trivet on stove top and cover with larger pan. Cook about 1 hour until set. Serve with lots of butter. Serves 4 to 6.

George Washington's Hoecakes

Legend says that slaves baked hoecakes on the back of a hoe over open fires. George Washington often ate three small hoecakes with tea for his breakfast at 7:00 A.M. He liked them with butter, maple syrup, or honey.

Coarse cornmeal   1 cup
Salt   ½ teaspoon
Shortening   1 tablespoon, melted
Hot water
Butter or margarine
Butter, maple syrup, or honey   topping

Mix cornmeal with salt and shortening. Add enough hot water to make dough that holds its shape, then shape into cakes. Rub with butter and cook directly on stove top or on hot griddle or skillet on stove top. Add butter when done and serve hot. Serves 2.

Yeast Sally Lunn

Is "Sally Lunn" named for the woman who first made this bread or a description of a bread that bursts forth (Sally) into a curved shape (Lunn)? Whatever the origins, it is a sumptuous tea cake served at Virginia country breakfasts. The following recipe is a variation of the one cooked by Dorothea Dandridge for her husband Patrick Henry at their home in Red Hill, Virginia, where he lived after retiring from the governorship and a career filled with fiery words—"Give me liberty or give me death."

Milk 1 cup
Butter ⅓ cup
Sugar 2 tablespoons
Salt 1 teaspoon
Yeast 2 teaspoons
Warm water ¼ cup
Eggs 3
Flour 4 cups

Scald milk and while hot, add butter, sugar, and salt. Cool until tepid. Dissolve yeast in warm water. Beat eggs until light. Combine milk mixture, yeast, and eggs. Add enough flour to make stiff batter. Beat thoroughly and set aside to rise near stove 30 minutes. Beat down vigorously. Repeat rising and beating down process several times. Pour into greased tube pan and let sit for about 1 hour until batter doubles in size. Put pan on trivet on stove top. Cover with larger pan and let cook about 1 hour until it sounds hollow to a thump. Serves 8.
Note: In a conventional oven, bake at 350° for about 60 minutes.

Griddle Scones

King William of Britain indirectly sent scones to America in the 1690s when he booted the Scots off their highlands to make way for sheep. Displaced small landowners hopscotched to America via Ireland, seeking land in western Pennsylvania and frontier areas similar to their homelands. Wives came bearing cuisine secrets that made home where the transient Scots and Scotch-Irish found themselves. Scones were cooked in cast-iron spiders over open fires even before the cottage fireplace was built.

Butter or margarine ½ cup
Sugar ¼ cup
Salt ¼ teaspoon
Flour 2 cups
Baking powder 1 tablespoon
Raisins ½ cup (optional)
Sour milk ½ cup
Butter
Jam

Combine butter, sugar, and salt, and mix well. Sift flour and baking powder. Stir in raisins if desired. Add alternately with milk to butter and sugar. Handle as little as possible. Place on lightly floured board and pat ¾-inch. Cut in rounds. Put skillet on stove top and grease slightly. Put scones on hot skillet and cook 15 minutes or until each scone is set. Carefully flip and cook other side about 5 more minutes. Serve with butter and jam. Makes 12.
Note: On a conventional stove, cook at medium to medium-high heat for 10 minutes.

English Muffins

When the English came to America, they intended to acquire precious metals and exotic cargo from the Indians and return home in the same season. But treasures of the New World were to come only by patiently waiting for a crop of tobacco to ripen, so the Englishmen stayed. In 1619, the Virginia Company sought to soothe the stranded men by bringing a shipload of fair maidens. They graced our shores with a proper taste of the homeland—an English muffin.

Yeast 4 teaspoons
Warm water 1⅔ cups
Brown sugar 2 tablespoons
Salt 2 teaspoons
Wheat germ ¼ cup
Whole wheat flour 2 cups
Unbleached flour 2½ cups
Cornmeal ¼ cup

Combine yeast and water in a large bowl and let stand 10 minutes. Stir in next 4 ingredients and 1 cup unbleached flour. Add more unbleached flour until dough pulls from sides of bowl. Turn dough onto floured board and knead until dough bounces back to touch. Add more flour if necessary. Place dough in greased bowl, turn dough over, then cover to rise until double in bulk. Punch dough down and roll out ½-inch thick on board sprinkled with a very thin layer of cornmeal. Cut into 3-inch rounds. Spread out sheet of foil and sprinkle with a small amount of cornmeal. Place muffins on foil cornmeal side up and let rise 1 hour. Put foil on *hot* stove top. Cook about 15 minutes on 1 side. Gently turn to other side and cook 15 minutes or until muffins are set. Remove from stove top and cool on racks. Makes 12.

"Army Bisquits"

General George Armstrong Custer (1839–1876) campaigned throughout the West against Indians, uncooperative about the white man taking over their land. A flamboyant man, Custer set up camp with his wife (to give him comfort), several dogs (to provide sport), and a black cook (to make feasts). He ate these biscuits smothered with bacon gravy.

Flour 2 cups
Leavening or baking powder 3 teaspoons
Bacon grease 4 tablespoons
"Crick" water* ¾ cup
Bacon Gravy (see Index)

Combine flour and leavening and stir in grease until mixture is mealy. Add water, blend, and form into a ball. Knead 10 times on a floured board, then roll out ¾-inch thick. Cut into squares or rounds. Cover hot stove with foil. Place biscuits on foil and cook on 1 side about 10 minutes. Turn gently to cook on other side about 10 minutes until biscuit is set. Serve with bacon gravy. Makes 6.
* Water from a creek. Tap water may be substituted.
Note: Instead of using foil, heat a lightweight metal skillet or griddle until hot on stove top. Put biscuits in and cook on 1 side about 15 minutes. Flip and cook on other side about 15 minutes until biscuit is set.

Sourdough Biscuits

In the West, sourdough was an institution with transient gold miners, pioneers, and cowboys who wanted their daily bread flaky and tender rather than rock-hard. Crusty old men carried hunks of dough in their shirt pockets. Many a tin of sourdough hung over the stove of gold miners' cabins in the 1849 California gold rush. Chuck wagon cooks out on a cattle drive slept with their starter. And gold miners in the Alaskan Klondike in 1896 were called sourdoughs. Sourdough biscuits, cooked in a skillet or on sticks over the open fire, were essential.

Flour   1 cup
Baking powder   1 tablespoon
Salt   ½ teaspoon
Baking soda   ½ teaspoon
Sugar   ½ teaspoon
Shortening   ¼ cup
Sourdough Starter   1 cup
Butter or margarine   2 tablespoons melted

Stir together first 5 ingredients in mixing bowl. Cut in shortening with pastry blender or 2 knives until mixture resembles coarse cornmeal. Stir in starter. Gather dough into ball in bowl and knead about 30 seconds in bowl. Roll out ½-inch thick on floured board and cut into 2-inch rounds. Quickly coat each biscuit with butter. Put a skillet or cookie sheet on stove top to heat. When hot, put biscuits on it and cook about 15 minutes. Gently flip to other side and cook about 15 more minutes. Makes 12.
Note: On a conventional stove, cook at 425° for 12 minutes.

Sourdough Starter

Warm water   ½ cup
Dry yeast   2 teaspoons
Flour   ½ cup
Sugar   1 teaspoon
Water   ¼ cup
Flour   ¼ cup
Sugar   1 teaspoon
Water   1 cup
Flour   1 cup
Sugar   1 teaspoon

Combine first 4 ingredients in warm jar. Partially cover and set in warm (100°) place for 24 hours. Then add next 3 ingredients and return jar to warm place for another 24 hours. After that, remove amount needed for recipe, then add remaining ingredients, stir, and store.

Sourdough Pancakes

To share a sourdough starter is to start a friendship. One Baptist minister spread his starter around his congregation after he held a pancake breakfast. Then he told the story of his starter. In 1896, an Alaskan gave it to a gold miner who gave it to a Baptist missionary. Once when the missionary went away on a trip, a friend kept house for him and decided to tidy up for his return. He threw out the "sour cream." The missionary got home just in time to rescue his starter from the garbage. (They say it landed on a bed of clean lettuce leaves.) The missionary shared it with a minister who gave it to a member of his congregation who gave it to the Baptist minister who tells the story. And so on it goes.

Sourdough Starter (see Index) 1 cup
Warm milk 2 cups
Flour 2 cups
Eggs 3
Salt 1 teaspoon
Sugar 1 tablespoon
Baking soda 2 teaspoons
Oil 2 tablespoons
Sourdough Starter 1 cup

Mix starter, milk, and flour together. Cover with cloth and let sit overnight in a warm (85°) place. In a bowl, beat together next 5 ingredients. Fold in 1 cup starter from first mixture and let rest 5 or 10 minutes. Heat greased skillet or griddle on stove top. Put a spoonful of batter on griddle. When bubbles form and burst, flip to cook on other side. Serves 6.
Note: On a conventional stove, use a lower temperature or the pancakes will be doughy.

Danish Aebleskiver   (Pancake Balls)

Among the Danish immigrants to filter into America in the 1860s was six-year-old Edward W. Bok. From a confused lad unable to speak English, he became winner of the 1921 Pulitzer Prize for his autobiography and editor of the Ladies Home Journal—*the first magazine in the United States to have a million subscribers. During his thirty years as editor, he gave American readers their first advice column (which he wrote himself until he found the right woman writer) and raised the quality of American homes with actual house plans, flower garden layouts, and pictures to hang on the walls—*

reproductions of masterpieces printed on the magazine's four-color presses. He undertook causes of sex education and the evils of patent medicines. Like other Danish immigrants, he would have eaten Aebleskiver, sometimes called pancake balls or Danish doughnuts, for breakfast, lunch, or dessert.

Dry yeast   1 package
Warm milk   ¼ cup
Sugar   1 teaspoon
Flour   2 cups
Eggs   3, beaten
Milk   2 cups
Cardamom   ½ teaspoon
Lemon zest   1 teaspoon
Butter   ½ cup, melted
Jam or applesauce

In large bowl dissolve yeast in warm milk. Sift dry ingredients into bowl. Add eggs and milk and mix well. Mix in cardamom, zest, and butter. Let rise about 2 hours. Put greased skiver pan (cast-iron pan with round holes, available in import shops) on stove top to heat. Put 2 tablespoons of batter into each section of pan. When bottom is lightly brown, turn the balls and brown the top side. Serve hot with jam or applesauce. Makes 2 dozen.

Potato Dumplings

Tobacco was the New World's gift to Old World aristocrats, but potatoes were the gift to peasants. American Indians had grown the potata *for centuries before English explorer Sir Francis Drake took it to Europe in the late seventeenth century. Today in Hirschhorn, Germany, there is a statue inscribed "To God and Francis Drake, who brought to Europe for the everlasting benefit of the poor—the Potato."*

Potatoes   1 cup peeled, cooked, mashed, and cooled
Bread crumbs   ½ cup
Parsley   1 tablespoon chopped
Egg   1
Salt and pepper   to taste

Mix ingredients and shape into walnut-sized balls. Drop into boiling water and boil about 10 minutes until cooked through.

Crullers

French hunters followed buffalo and Indian paths into the Cumberland River area to trap the skins and furs of animals attracted there by the natural salt lick—thus French Lick, now Nashville. Timothy Demonbreun was the first white man brave enough to settle in those Tennessee hills. More settlers joined him in the late 1700s. They wrote the Cumberland Compact, the first written constitutional government west of the Alleghenies. At Demonbreun's home in 1802, the board of commissioners met to adopt some police regulations for loitering slaves and stray hogs, because the area was becoming more populated and needed order. They may have eaten a few crullers, a light French pastry that the French Heritage Society today attributes to Demonbreun.

Sugar ¾ cup
Shortening ⅓ cup
Eggs 2
Salt 1 teaspoon
Nutmeg ¼ teaspoon
Cinnamon ½ teaspoon
Baking powder 4 teaspoons
Milk 1 cup
Flour 4 cups
Oil to fry
Powdered sugar to coat crullers

Cream sugar, shortening, and eggs. Add salt, nutmeg, cinnamon, and baking powder. Add milk alternately with flour. Mix well. Roll out dough 1-inch thick on floured board. Cut into strips 1¾-inches wide and 3 inches long. Make 2 lengthwise scores in each. Heat fresh oil in iron skillet. Place dough into oil a few pieces at a time. Turn over when brown on one side. Cook until done. Drain on towel. Sprinkle with powdered sugar. Makes 2 dozen.

Halloween Bread

Pumpkins carved with triangular eyes and frightful mouths glare from the porches of millions of American homes on Halloween. We get this custom from an Irish fable that tells of a man named Jack who could not enter heaven because he was so miserly and could not enter hell because he played practical jokes on the devil. So he walked the earth with his lantern until Judgment Day. Rather than leave the jack-o'-lantern to rot into mush, be just a little bit miserly and use it in this recipe from Virginia's Roanoke Valley.

Shortening ⅔ cup
Brown sugar 2 cups
Granulated sugar ⅔ cup
Eggs 4
Pumpkin 2 cups cooked
Water ⅔ cup
Flour 3⅓ cups
Baking soda 2 teaspoons
Salt 1½ teaspoons
Baking powder ½ teaspoon
Cinnamon 1 teaspoon
Cloves 1 teaspoon
Ginger ¼ teaspoon
Pecans or walnuts 1 cup coarsely chopped
Golden seedless raisins 1 cup

Cream shortening and sugars together. Beat in eggs, pumpkin, and water. Blend dry ingredients and spices, add to creamed mixture, and mix well. Add nuts and raisins and stir. Pour into 2 greased 1-pound coffee cans, cover with foil, and tie with string. Place cans on rack in kettle and pour in water to reach one-fourth up the side of each can. Steam bread 1½ to 2 hours until it begins to pull away from sides of each can. When done, remove from kettle and let stand on racks 5 minutes. Remove from cans. Makes 2 loaves.
Note: On a conventional stove, bake at 350° for 1 hour and 15 minutes.

Lefse

Lutherans from Norway swept into the northwest United States in the 1800s, lured by visions of "wheat bread every day and pork at least three times a week!" Their farms, etched by their strength and piety from unbroken prairie sod, often produced little. Their ingenuity turned potatoes into a stomach-filling delicacy called lefse. "New Norway" stretched from Wisconsin and Minnesota to the Dakotas and the Pacific coast where at Pacific Lutheran University in Tacoma, Washington, one hears the football cheer:

> *Lutefisk, lutefisk, lefse, lefse,*
> *Ve're the mighty Luterans,*
> *Ya, sure, ya betcha!*

Salt 1 teaspoon
Sugar 1 tablespoon
Shortening 2 tablespoons, melted
Whipping cream ½ cup
Potatoes 3 cups peeled, cooked, riced, and cooled
Flour 3 cups sifted
Butter ½ cup
Sugar ½ cup
Cinnamon 2 teaspoons

Gradually add first 4 ingredients to potatoes. Add 2 cups flour. Continue to add more flour until you can roll dough out without its sticking to the board. Use a pastry cloth, if desired. Roll out into 12 by 12-inch squares, very thin like a piecrust. Cover stove top with foil or cook directly on the stove. Put the round dough on the *hot* surface. Bake quickly on 1 side until lightly browned. Turn and cook other side. Cool separately on dish towels. Freeze for later use or serve cut in wedges, spread with a mixture of butter, sugar, and cinnamon and rolled up like a crescent roll. Makes 5 dozen.
Note: Instead of a wood stove, a hot grill or lefse iron set at 375° to 400° can be used.

Sweets

Desserts to us are calorie-filled fluffs eaten at the end of a meal. But desserts of yesteryear transformed cornmeal, bread crumbs, hearty indigenous sweetenings, and fruits into healthy treats that could even be part of the main course. They were filled with spices—to camouflage the smoky taste of drafty open fires—and steamed on the stove top, in many cases, since for many years only the elite owned ovens. These desserts were a lesson in frugality.

Lemon Custard

Turn-of-the-century logging camps served bountiful meals of 9,500 calories per day per logger. The "wild and wooly, never-been-curried-above-the-knees" loggers were apt to move from camp to camp to find the cook who served the best coffee and made the best lemon pie before they started felling timber. The Tilton River camp of L.T. Murray in Washington attracted a lot of loggers—and Murray's friends as well—with the wares of pastry chef Mildred Chambers. In a day, she baked seventy-five dozen cookies and made forty to fifty pies—often with this lemon custard filling.

Eggs   4, well beaten
Lemon rind   of 2 lemons, grated
Lemon juice   1 tablespoon
Sugar   8 tablespoons
Cornstarch   2 tablespoons
Water   3 tablespoons
Butter   ¼ cup, melted
Sour cream   1 cup, sweetened with sugar

One at a time, mix together the eggs, lemon rind, lemon juice, sugar, cornstarch, water, and butter. Pour mixture into top of double boiler and place in bottom of double boiler filled with 2 inches of water. Stir well and cover. Place on stove top and cook about 1 hour until custard is cooked through, and knife comes out clean. Serve with sour cream. Serves 6.

Apple Custard

Johnny Appleseed (1774–1845) wanders into our imaginations wearing an eccentric smile and a tattered coffee-sack shirt. Indeed, John Chapman, alias Appleseed, was an altruistic New Englander who at age twenty-three scavenged apple seeds from cider presses and spread seedlings across the Ohio River Valley. When ambitious men of his day were acquiring large tracts of free western land, he was a nurseryman selling seedlings and seeds to frontier settlers at little or no cost. This was in keeping with his beliefs as a Swedenborgian. To him, nature was related to the spiritual world, which was not in the sky but inside himself to be lived in the earthly life. Spreading apple trees so people could enjoy treats like this custard of the times was how Mr. Chapman lived his religion.

Egg yolks   6
Sugar   ½ cup
Applesauce   1 cup
Lemon zest   1 teaspoon
Milk   1 cup
Apple   1, sliced
Salt   ½ teaspoon
Water   1 cup
Whipped cream   topping

Put egg yolks, sugar, and applesauce in saucepan and place on stove top. Stir mixture until smooth. Add lemon zest and milk and continue simmering over low heat. Place on a trivet and stir until custard thickens. Pour into custard cups. Soak apples in saltwater 5 minutes. Drain and garnish custard. Top with whipped cream. Serves 4.

Apple Compote

This recipe came from both the German section of the 1930 Kentucky Home Cookbook *and an immigrant who came by plane only a decade ago. A version of baked apples, this recipe epitomizes the everyday best in wood heat stove cookery.*

Rome apples   1 for each person
Cold water
Lemon juice   1 tablespoon
Currant jelly or sweet marmalade   1 cup
Raisins   ¼ cup (optional)
White wine   1 cup
Water
Sugar   1 cup
Lemon peel   of ½ lemon, thinly sliced
Sugar   ¼ cup

Peel apples and remove core without removing 1 end. Soak in cold water with lemon juice for 15 minutes. Fill cavities with jelly, and raisins if desired, and place in stewing pan. Pour in wine and enough water to fill pan without touching the apple filling. Add sugar and lemon peel to water. Cover and place on back of stove top to stew until apples are tender. To serve, remove apples to dish. Add additional sugar to liquor in pan and let boil down to jelly consistency. Pour this over apples on platter. Serves 4.

Cherry Michel

Once upon a time an Oregon girl married a German boy and they had at least one thing in common—cherries. The luscious red fruit grows profusely in both the Rhineland and the Willamette Valley, so the couple combined them with bread crumbs for this economical delight. (Germans serve it as a luncheon main dish with salad; Americans can serve it as a dessert.) To the couple who gave me this recipe, introduced me to the wood stove's rich history, and showed me how to sweep a chimney—may life ever be a bowl full of cherries.

Butter ⅓ cup
Sugar ½ cup
Eggs 6, separated
Lemon zest of 1 lemon
Cinnamon ¼ teaspoon
Bread or cracker crumbs 2 cups
Pie cherries 1 cup pitted

Cream butter and sugar together. In another bowl beat together egg yolks, lemon zest, and cinnamon. Add to creamed mixture. Gently stir in crumbs, then add cherries. Beat egg whites until frothy and fold gently into mixture. Pour into greased 1½-quart baking dish. Put on trivet and cover with large pan. Cook about 1 hour until knife comes out clean. Serves 8 to 10.

Gingerbread

Honyockers—homesteaders on the northern Great Plains of Montana between 1910 and 1920—were the subject of a cruel practical joke. They fell victim to overly optimistic rainfall reports and developers' propaganda that Montana soil was so rich you deposited it by the bag straight into the bank. Clerks, bankers, and factory hands rented a freight car for fifty dollars and left the city to become farmers and ranchers. They awaited the rains that never came and watched the soil blow away. With the "mares dead on the range and the colt in the same condition... what is to be done?" They left the land. The honyockers faced odds even more appalling than those faced by earlier pioneers. This moist Montana recipe is a tribute to the brave spirit of those twentieth century pioneers and others with broken dreams to rebuild.

Butter ½ cup
Brown sugar ½ cup
Eggs 2
Molasses 1 cup

Cloves ½ teaspoon
Allspice ½ teaspoon
Nutmeg ½ teaspoon
Cinnamon 1 teaspoon
Ginger 1¼ teaspoons
Salt ½ teaspoon
Baking powder 1 teaspoon
Baking soda 1 teaspoon
Flour 2½ cups
Hot water 1 cup

Cream butter and brown sugar together. Beat in eggs and molasses. Stir in cloves, allspice, nutmeg, cinnamon, ginger, salt, baking powder, and baking soda. Stir in flour, then hot water and beat well. Pour into 2 greased 5 by 9-inch loaf pans. Place pans on trivets on stove top and cover with inverted roasting pan or other large pan. Bake about 1½ hours or until broom straw comes out clean.
Note: In a conventional oven, bake at 350° for 50 minutes.

Dutch-Oven Gingerbread

Cakes cooked on an open hearth absorbed the taste of smoke from the draft that swept into the pot when the lid was lifted or not tightly sealed. Ginger helped to camouflage the unpleasant taste. This gingerbread comes out moist and full of desirable flavor from cooking in the tight pot atop the stove.

Flour 2 cups
Salt ¼ teaspoon
Ginger 1 teaspoon
Cinnamon 1 teaspoon
Baking soda 1 teaspoon
Sugar ½ cup
Orange zest 1 tablespoon
Egg 1
Molasses ½ cup
Butter ¼ cup
Hot water ½ cup

Mix dry ingredients together, then add remaining ingredients. Pour into greased Dutch oven. Place on trivet on hot stove top. Bake about 45 minutes until broom straw comes out clean. Serves 6.

Gingerbread-Applesauce Pudding Cake

Explorers searched faraway places and opened America for settlement in their search for spices—especially ginger, which was valued for toothaches and indigestion. Even before the Norman Conquest of England, ginger was the most common of spices except pepper, and Chaucer spoke of gingerbread in the thirteenth century. By the sixteenth century it was a favored gift fit for a slave to give his king, who served it with cream and a baked apple. Gingerbread cooked with applesauce makes a moist pudding that has survived from the colonial hearth to contemporary campground cookery.

Applesauce 4 cups
Sugar ½ cup
Shortening ½ cup
Molasses ½ cup
Eggs 2
Unbleached white flour 1 cup
Whole wheat flour ½ cup
Salt ½ teaspoon
Baking soda 1 teaspoon
Ginger 1 teaspoon
Cinnamon 1 teaspoon
Sour milk ½ cup

Put applesauce in bottom of Dutch oven or 3-quart covered pan. Cream sugar and shortening. Add molasses and mix well. Drop in eggs 1 at a time and beat well after each addition. Sift together next 6 ingredients and add alternately with milk to first mixture, stirring until well blended. Pour batter over applesauce and spread. Cover pot and put on trivet on stove top. Cook about 1 hour until broom straw comes out clean. Serves 8.
Note: In a conventional oven, bake at 350° for 45 minutes.

Apple Charlotte

Patrick Henry's granddaughter carried on her grandfather's fiery public spirit through the pages of a cookbook. Marion Cabell Tyree collected and edited some 250 recipes of well-known homemakers in order to present the purest examples of domestic principles and practices to others. Her purpose during the Reconstruction period after the Civil War was to make "American homes more attractive to American husbands and spare them a resort to hotels and saloons...." This Apple Charlotte, a perfect example of a pudding, exemplifies southern cooking—a blend of New England thrift and Carolina casualness at its best.

Stewed apples (see Index) 2 cups
Whole wheat bread crumbs 2 cups
Butter 1 tablespoon, melted
Red wine 1 tablespoon
Cinnamon 1 teaspoon
Nutmeg ¼ teaspoon freshly grated
Lemon zest of 1 lemon
Eggs 3, beaten
Brown sugar 1 cup, packed
Heavy cream

Mix together apples and bread crumbs. Stir in butter, wine, cinnamon, nutmeg, lemon, eggs, and brown sugar. Blend well. Pour into buttered 2-quart baking dish and tightly cover with foil. Set on trivet on stove top and cook several hours or overnight on a closed down stove until a knife blade comes out clean. Serve with heavy cream for breakfast or dessert. Serves 8.
Note: In a conventional oven, bake at 250° for 3 hours.

Cinnamon Pudding

Cinnamon scented holy places in Old Testament days and appeased the gods of ancient Rome. This pudding, which uses the ancient spice, came to America with a religious group—Mennonites of Berne, Switzerland, who moved their entire community to Berne, Indiana, in the 1800s.

Sugar 1 cup
Butter 2 tablespoons
Baking powder 2 teaspoons
Flour 2 cups
Cinnamon 1 teaspoon
Milk 1 cup
Brown sugar 1½ cups
Water 1½ cups
Butter 2 tablespoons
Raisins ½ cup
Nuts ½ cup chopped

Mix together first 6 ingredients. Put into greased 9 by 13-inch baking pan. Boil next 3 ingredients in a saucepan. Pour over batter in pan. Sprinkle with raisins and nuts. Set pan on trivet on stove top and cover with a larger baking pan. Cook about 1 hour until knife comes out clean. Serves 6 to 8.
Note: In a conventional oven, bake at 375° for 30 minutes.

Rice Pudding

Civil war might well rage in the United States among nationalities that claim to have originated rice pudding. Riso *in Italian,* reis *in German,* riz *in French,* arroz *in Spanish, and* rice *in English—it was the most familiar of cereal grains in the known world at one time. Rice was available in America from the earliest days of settlement because a trading vessel from Madagascar was forced to take refuge in the Charleston, South Carolina, harbor in 1693. The ship's captain sold a small bag of seed rice to a merchant and by 1700 rice had thrived and become "Carolina gold." At the end of a meal, this rice dessert satisfies—in any language.*

Milk 1 quart
Sugar 5 tablespoons
Rice 5 tablespoons uncooked
Egg 1
Butter 1 tablespoon
Vanilla 1 teaspoon
Raisins 1 cup (optional) or
    Crushed pineapple 8-ounce can, drained (optional)
Cinnamon garnish

Combine milk, sugar, and rice in heavy saucepan and cover pan. Place on trivet and simmer about 30 minutes until rice is tender. Remove pan from heat and cool about 5 minutes. Beat egg and add 1 tablespoon rice mixture. Return egg and rice mixture to saucepan and stir, cooking until mixture thickens. Remove from stove and stir in butter and vanilla. Stir in raisins if desired, and sprinkle top with cinnamon. Serves 4.

Indiana Persimmon Pudding

One must be properly introduced to the persimmon. When not fully ripe, it "will draw a man's mouth awrie with much torment," wrote English explorer John Smith in his seventeenth-century report of the New World. But when fully ripe it is "delicious as an Apricock." Settlers from Virginia, Kentucky, Tennessee, the Carolinas, and Maryland moved into Indiana when it became a state in 1816 and discovered wild persimmons growing in abundance. This recipe is one of the best they developed.

Persimmon pulp 2 cups
Sugar ½ cup
Butter ½ cup
Brown sugar ¾ cup
Eggs 2
Milk 1 cup
Cinnamon 1 teaspoon
Baking soda ½ teaspoon
Salt pinch
Baking powder 1 teaspoon
Flour 2 scant cups
Whipped cream

Thoroughly mix ingredients, except cream, in order given. Pour into an oiled 1½-quart baking dish or pudding mold. Cover tightly with foil and tie with string, or use a tight-fitting lid. Place on a rack in a steamer kettle containing 1 inch of water. Steam about 45 to 60 minutes until pudding is set or knife comes out clean. Cool, then serve with whipped cream. Serves 10.
Note: In a conventional oven, bake at 350° for 45 minutes.

Cranberry Pudding

Another name for this dessert might be "peace pudding." The cranberry was an Indian peace symbol. A Delaware chief named Pakimintzen, "Cranberry Eater," passed out cranberries at tribal peace feasts. Colonists tried the same tactic when they sent ten barrels of cranberries to soothe angry King Charles II when they minted their own coins. Indians and colonists mixed cranberries into sun-dried cakes called pemmican. This glorified version of that crude cake substitutes butter for deer fat and lightens it with leavening. Otherwise it is a taste straight from the colonial hearth.

Butter or margarine ¼ cup
Brown sugar ½ cup
Honey 1 cup
Eggs 4, beaten
Fresh cranberries ¾ cup, chopped
Flour 3 cups
Baking powder 3 teaspoons
Salt 1 teaspoon
Whipped cream

Cream butter, sugar, and honey in large bowl. Mix with eggs and cranberries. Sift dry ingredients, then gradually blend into first mixture. Pour into a greased and floured 1½-quart pudding mold or baking dish. Cover tightly with foil and tie with string, or use a tight-fitting lid. Place on rack in large steamer kettle and pour in water to reach halfway up the side of the mold. Cover kettle and steam gently 2 hours or until knife comes out clean. Cool slightly, unmold onto platter, and serve with whipped cream. Serves 6.

Plum Pudding

The potato famine that hit Ireland in the 1840s brought Irishmen to America to escape starvation. In their humble shanties, the fruity aroma of this pudding as it steamed in huge black pots over open fires was the same as it had been back home in their cottages.

Cinnamon   1 teaspoon
Ground cloves   ½ teaspoon
Nutmeg   ½ teaspoon
Mace   dash
Salt   pinch
Flour   ½ cup
Fresh bread crumbs   at least 1½ cups
Suet   1½ cups
Brown sugar   ¾ cup
Eggs   5
Large baking apple   1, peeled and grated
Orange juice   at least ¼ cup
Currants   1 cup
Raisins   1 cup
Candied citrus peel   ½ cup chopped

Combine first 6 ingredients, then mix in bread crumbs. Mix together suet and sugar. Beat in eggs and add apple and orange juice. Thoroughly mix dry ingredients and egg mixture in large bowl. Add more bread crumbs or juice to make a stiff batter. Add currants, raisins, and peel. Pour into a greased 2-quart pudding dish. Cover tightly with foil and tie with string. Place on rack in steamer kettle and add water to reach halfway up side of dish. Cover kettle and simmer 6 hours. Remove pudding from dish, cool, then store in cool place until ready to use. Ages well in 1 month. Serves 12.

Date Pudding

Since the first date palms were transplanted in tubs from Egypt to Salt River Valley, Arizona, in 1890, dates have been naturalized in our diet. A fruit of Biblical times, dates were popular with Old Order Mennonites—called "House Amish" because they met in homes rather than a church. From a score of their date pudding recipes, we chose this one.

Brown sugar   2 cups
Butter   4 tablespoons softened
Flour   1 cup sifted
Salt   ½ teaspoon
Baking powder   1 teaspoon
Milk   ½ cup
Dates   ¾ cup chopped
Pecans or walnuts   ¾ cup chopped
Boiling water   1½ cups
Granulated sugar   ½ cup
Vanilla   ½ teaspoon
Butter   2 tablespoons

Mix together brown sugar and 4 tablespoons butter. Sift flour, salt, and baking powder together and add to sugar mixture. Stir in milk, dates, and nuts. Pour into greased 8-inch cake pan. Combine remaining ingredients and pour over batter in pan. Place on trivet on stove top and cover with roasting pan. Bake about an hour until pudding is cooked through and a knife comes out clean. Serves 8.
Note: In a conventional oven, bake at 350° for 40 minutes.

Blueberry Steamed Pudding

One evening I impulsively took a basket of fresh blueberries to my dinner hostess, whom I had never met. Elizabeth Coville must have thought that I knew all about her grandfather Frederick V. Coville. He had tamed the wild American blueberry when others had failed because he cultivated the blueberry in highly acid soil rather than in the rich garden soil. In doing so, he put the large plump berry into our muffins and pancakes. He predicted it would outdistance the cranberry in our diet: "You can't use cranberries without buying a turkey to eat with them." This recipe alone proves the blueberry's worth.

Blueberries 2 cups
Flour 1 tablespoon
Butter ¼ cup, softened
Sugar ¾ cup
Egg 1, well beaten
Vanilla ½ teaspoon
Lemon zest 1 tablespoon
Flour 2¼ cups sifted
Baking soda ½ teaspoon
Buttermilk 1 cup
Whipped cream topping

Toss berries with 1 tablespoon flour. Cream butter and sugar in bowl until fluffy. Beat in egg, then vanilla and lemon zest. Combine 2¼ cups flour and baking soda. Alternately add flour and buttermilk to butter and sugar mixture, blend well, and fold in berries. Turn into a greased and floured 1½-quart souffle dish and smooth out top. Cover with foil, tie with string, and set on rack in steamer kettle. Add water to kettle to reach 1 inch from top of dish. Cover kettle and simmer on stove about 3 hours. When knife comes out clean, remove dish from kettle. Run knife around edge of pudding and invert on serving platter. Serve warm with whipped cream. Serves 6.

Original Indian Pudding

Indians had cornmeal. White men had molasses and ginger. They mixed them together to create a taste of friendship.

Milk 1 quart
Molasses ½ cup
Coarse cornmeal 5 tablespoons
Salt ½ teaspoon
Ginger 1 teaspoon

Scald milk in saucepan on stove top and stir in molasses. Combine cornmeal, salt, and ginger, and stir thoroughly into milk. Remove from heat, pour into greased 1½-quart baking dish, cover with foil, and tie with string. Place dish on rack in kettle containing 1½ inches of water. Cover kettle and steam pudding for several hours until knife comes out clean. Serves 6 to 8.
Variation: For Blackstone Pudding, chop 2 medium cooking apples, then stir into pudding.
Note: In a conventional oven, bake at 275° for 3 hours.

Indian Pudding

Changed but cherished through the years, Indian pudding was one of Mrs. Woodrow Wilson's choice dishes when she went to live in the White House on 4 March 1913. Her one regret in accepting the honor of first lady was that she would have less time to oversee her family's meals and cook this pudding.

Stone-ground yellow cornmeal*   1 cup
Molasses   ½ cup
Sugar   ¼ cup
Butter   ¼ cup
Baking soda   ¼ teaspoon
Egg yolk   1
Ginger   ½ teaspoon
Cinnamon   ¼ teaspoon
Nutmeg   ¼ teaspoon
Hot milk   1½ cups
Whipped cream

Mix all ingredients except half of the milk and the cream and bring to a simmer. Stir in remaining milk. Pour into greased 1-quart pudding dish. Cover with foil, tie with string, and put on rack in steamer kettle containing 1 inch of water. Steam 5 to 7 hours. Serve warm with whipped cream. Serves 6 to 8.

* Stone-ground cornmeal is fragile, because the germ is still intact, and should be refrigerated or kept in a cool place.

Note: In a conventional oven, bake at 275° for 3 hours.

Carrot Pudding

One of the largest producers of gunpowder this side of the Atlantic was the du Pont factory in Delaware's Brandywine Valley. Government contracts during the War of 1812 expanded the company, but European shareholders were not receiving the dividends they expected. They sent the 24-year-old son of a Swiss investor to investigate. Antoine Bidermann stayed on to help run the company and marry the daughter of owner Éluthère Irénée du Pont. Disturbed by injuries from the frequent explosions that occurred in the powder mills when the workers mixed together the sulfur, charcoal, and saltpeter, Bidermann introduced the radical policy of pensions for families of victims. Winterthur, the home built by Bidermann and his wife Evalina, today holds over 70,000 examples of American decorative art and serves this carrot pudding, an edible antique of the eighteenth and nineteenth centuries, to museum visitors.

Eggs 4
Sugar 1½ cups
Oil 1½ cups
Vanilla 2 teaspoons
Flour 2 cups
Baking soda 2 teaspoons
Salt ½ teaspoon
Cinnamon 2 teaspoons
Carrots 2 cups peeled and grated
Raisins ½ cup
Nuts ½ cup chopped
Cream cheese

Beat eggs and sugar until light and fluffy. Add oil and vanilla. Beat well. Sift flour with baking soda, salt, and cinnamon. Add to sugar mixture. Beat well. Stir in carrots, raisins, and nuts. Pour into a greased 2½-quart baking dish. Place on trivet on stove top and cover with inverted roasting pan. Bake several hours or overnight until knife comes out clean. Spread with cream cheese when cool. Serves 8 to 10.

Roly-Poly Pudding

Four countries claimed the territory between Spanish California and Russian Alaska in the early 1800s. By 1825, the British had gained a stronghold with the Hudson Bay Company's fur headquarters at Fort Vancouver on the Columbia River; and the Americans had gained ground with the Lewis and Clark Expedition of 1804, sent out by President Thomas Jefferson, and with the Methodist missionaries who slipped in under the cross in 1834. Tension was high in 1844 when James K. Polk campaigned for president with the famous claim to Oregon, "Fifty-Four Forty or Fight." But a treaty in 1846 divided British and American claims to the Oregon Territory at the 49th parallel. Had things gone otherwise, this English pastry—chronicled in one of the delightful children's books of English writer Beatrix Potter—might have enjoyed more popularity in America.

Flour   1 cup sifted
Salt   ½ teaspoon
Baking powder   ½ teaspoon
Cinnamon   ½ teaspoon
Sugar   1 tablespoon
Butter   3 tablespoons
Milk   ⅓ cup
Butter   2 tablespoons, melted
Jam, peach or cherry   ½ cup
Custard Sauce

Combine flour, salt, baking powder, cinnamon, and sugar in a large bowl. Cut in butter with 2 knives or pastry blender. Stir in milk. Knead and roll to ⅓-inch thickness on floured board. Brush pastry with butter. Place jam on pastry and gently roll up. Place seam down in a greased 8-inch square cake pan. Place pan on trivet on stove top and cover with inverted roasting pan. Bake about 1 hour until pastry is cooked through. Serve warm with Custard Sauce. Serves 6 to 8.
Note: In a conventional oven, bake at 425° for 30 minutes.

Custard Sauce

Eggs   2, beaten
Sugar   ½ cup
Salt   dash
Milk   2 cups, scalded
Vanilla   ½ teaspoon

Mix together eggs, sugar, and salt. Pour in milk, stirring constantly. Cook mixture in top of double boiler until custard coats a spoon. When cool, add vanilla. Makes 1 pint.

Maple Bread Pudding

Maple syrup is America's own sweetening. Legend has it that an Indian woman was boiling her moose meat in maple tree sap and got distracted. When she came back to her pot, the meat was sitting in maple syrup.

Currants ⅓ cup
Orange juice 2 tablespoons
Bread 4 slices, buttered and cubed
Pecans, walnuts, or almonds ½ cup
Lemon or orange zest 2 tablespoons
Maple syrup ⅔ cup or
    Brown sugar 1 cup and
    Water ¼ cup
Eggs 2
Milk 1½ cups
Light cream ½ cup
Salt ¼ teaspoon
Vanilla 1 teaspoon
Cream topping

Soak currants in orange juice. Arrange half the bread, drained currants (reserve juice), nuts, and zest on bottom of greased Dutch oven. Drizzle half the syrup over the bread. Repeat these layers. Beat together remaining ingredients (except cream for topping) and orange juice from currants. Pour over layered ingredients. Set on trivet, cover, and bake about an hour until pudding is puffy and done. Serve with cream. Serves 6.
Note: Put pudding in a greased 1-quart pudding mold instead of a Dutch oven. Tightly cover dish. Place in steamer kettle with water 1-inch deep and steam 2 hours.

Chocolate Pudding

Dr. James Baker set up the first American chocolate processing company in Massachusetts in 1765 to make medicine. Chocolate was considered an aphrodisiac as well. So this luscious steamed dessert should be "good for what ails you."

Butter or margarine ½ cup
Brown sugar 1½ cups
Vanilla 2 teaspoons
Eggs 2
Unbleached flour 2⅓ cups
Cocoa ¾ cup
Water ½ cup
Orange juice 1 cup
Baking soda 1 teaspoon
Nuts ½ cup chopped
Raspberry jam
Whipped cream

Cream butter, sugar, and vanilla together in large bowl. Add eggs and beat well. Combine flour and cocoa. Combine water and orange juice and stir in baking soda. Add flour and liquid mixtures alternately to butter and sugar, then stir in nuts. Pour into well-greased 2-quart baking dish or mold. Cover with greased foil, tie with string, and put on rack in steamer kettle containing 1 inch of water. Steam about 2 to 3 hours until broom straw comes out clean. Cool, unmold, spread with jam, and serve with whipped cream. Serves 10 to 12.

Variation: Pour half of batter into baking dish. Lay slices of cream cheese over that and pour in remaining batter. Cook as above.

Apple Pandowdy

Pandowdy preceded shallow pies in preoven days. Cooks put pastry over apples because it held in their flavor and moisture and tasted better than apples cooked in an open pan. Toward the end of cooking, they "dowdied" the crust with a sharp knife, then flipped the pan upside down onto a platter so the apples and juice oozed over the pastry. Except for the influx of ovens into our kitchens that began in 1845, we might quip "as American as apple pandowdy."

Pastry   for two 9-inch crusts
Butter   4 tablespoons, melted
Sugar   ½ cup
Cinnamon   ½ teaspoon
Nutmeg   ¼ teaspoon
Salt   dash
Apples   10 cups thinly sliced
Molasses   ½ cup
Water   ¼ cup
Butter   3 tablespoons, melted
Heavy cream

Roll out pastry and brush with some of the 4 tablespoons butter. Fold in half, roll out again, and brush with more butter. Fold again and brush with remainder of the 4 tablespoons butter. Chill. Mix together sugar, spices, and salt. Toss with apple slices. Put apples in 13 by 9 by 2-inch dish. Combine molasses, water, and 3 tablespoons butter, and pour over apples. Roll out pastry to 15 by 11 inches. Place over apples, turn under edges, and flute. Set on trivet on stove top and cover with inverted larger pan. Let cook about an hour. "Dowdy" crust by cutting slits through the pastry. Cook another 20 minutes until apples are tender and invert on platter and serve with cream. Serves 6 to 8.
Note: In a conventional oven, bake at 350° for ½ hour.

Lemon Pot Pie

Christopher Columbus not only found us on 12 October in 1492, but he brought us the lemon, too. On his second sea voyage to Haiti under the Spanish flag, he brought a whole society in miniature—pigs, cows, priests, farmers, weavers, women, and lemon seed. By 1579 lemon trees flourished in St. Augustine, Florida, and their tart, delicious juice was cooked over the open fire into this forerunner of our pie.

Flour 1½ cups
Baking powder 3 teaspoons
Salt ⅛ teaspoon
Butter or margarine ½ cup
Water 3 cups
Sugar 1½ cups
Lemon juice of 3 lemons
Heavy cream

Sift flour, baking powder, and salt together. Cut in butter with 2 knives or a pastry cutter. Stir in 1 cup water to make a paste the consistency of cake batter. Put 2 cups water in heavy saucepan. Add sugar and lemon juice. Stir and simmer gently 20 to 30 minutes on back of stove until liquid thickens slightly. Drop spoonfuls of paste into simmering liquid, cover, and cook another 20 to 30 minutes until paste is set. Serve hot or cold with cream. Serves 8.

Blueberry Cobbler

Wild blueberries grew prolifically in New England pastures to be gathered for cobblers, deep dish pies that sealed in the luscious flavor with a one-crust top, jams, cakes, and puddings, or eaten fresh. One sixty-year-old man remembered in 1916 how he and his friends ate white blueberries from an albino bush down by their swimming hole.

Flour 2 cups
Sugar ¼ cup
Baking powder 4 teaspoons
Salt ½ teaspoon
Shortening ⅓ cup
Milk ½ cup
Egg 1, well beaten
Blueberries 2 cups
Sugar ¼ cup
Flour 2 tablespoons

Sift together first 4 ingredients. Cut in shortening with pastry blender or 2 knives. Add milk and egg and beat well. Put berries in 1½-quart pudding dish and stir in ¼ cup sugar and 2 tablespoons flour. Drop batter over berries. Cover dish with foil and tie with string. Put on rack in large kettle with 2 inches of water. Cover kettle. Put on stove top and let cook about an hour until broom straw inserted in batter comes out clean and berries are cooked down. Serves 8.

Shaker Apple Dumplings

When Shakers in South Union, Kentucky, received a cookstove as a gift from their brothers and sisters in Ohio, they wrote in their journal of May 1929, "This day is famous as having the first cooking stove in our kitchen . . . " Although it was no more than the heat stoves we have today, it gave relief from laborious fireplace cookery. Shakers designed a simple, efficient stove so typical of their thrift and ingenuity that today it has been adopted as an official symbol in Shakertown at South Union. Travelers or Society members ate apple dumplings along with roast wild turkey, fried ham, fried potatoes, cushaw squash, and hoecakes.

Pastry   for two 9-inch crusts
Large tart apples   4, peeled and cored
Sugar or honey   ½ cup
Heavy cream   2 tablespoons
Rosewater*   1 tablespoon (optional)
Hot maple syrup   ½ cup

Roll pastry until thin and cut in 4 squares large enough to wrap around each apple. Place apple in center of each pastry square. Thoroughly mix together sugar, cream, and rosewater, if desired, and fill apples. Bring corners of pastry squares together and wet edges so they cling together. Prick pastry with fork. Place in Dutch oven or covered saucepan and cook about 1 hour until syrup thickens and apples are tender. Baste with syrup. Makes 4.
* An essence high in vitamin C that results from soaking seed pods of wild roses.
Note: In a conventional oven, bake at 350° for 30 minutes.

Green-Tomato Mincemeat Turnovers

Turnovers fried in a spider over red-hot coals pocketed a sweet or meat as in this recipe, similar to Shaker-period recipes. It was discovered both in an old Kentucky farm journal and in Maine recipe records by Mrs. Elizabeth Kremer, food director of Shakertown at Pleasant Hill, Kentucky. To make the mincemeat filling, choose a cold day when heating season has started and green tomatoes otherwise would be wasted, a deed unthinkable to the Shakers, who wasted nothing.

Small green tomatoes   3 pounds
Water
Green apples   3 pounds
Seedless raisins   2 pounds
Cider vinegar   1 cup
Cloves   2 tablespoons
Dark brown sugar   4 pounds
Cinnamon   1 tablespoon
Salt   2 tablespoons
Nutmeg   1 tablespoon
Orange zest   of 1 orange (optional)
Pastry
Butter   1 tablespoon to each quart of mincemeat
Apple   1, chopped (optional)

Core and chop tomatoes. Drain over bowl and measure juice, then discard juice. Measure amount of water equivalent to juice. In a large kettle, combine tomatoes and water. Boil mixture, drain over bowl, and measure juice. Add water equal to tomato juice discarded. Do this a total of 3 times. Peel, core, and chop apples. Again drain tomatoes, return to kettle, and add remaining ingredients except pastry, butter, and apple. Boil slowly until mixture is clear and thickened to marmalade consistency. Pour into hot, sterilized ½- to 1-pint jars and seal with boiled canning lids. (Makes 3 quarts.) When ready to make turnovers, mix butter with mincemeat and add apple if desired. Roll pastry out to ¼-inch thickness, then cut into six 4-inch circles. Place 1 tablespoon mincemeat in center, fold over, fasten edges with fork and pierce with fork. Slightly grease bottom of skillet. Fry turnover on one side until brown and flip to brown other side. Makes 6 turnovers.

Pastry

Flour 1 cup
Salt ½ teaspoon
Baking powder 1½ teaspoons
Shortening 3 tablespoons
Milk 6 tablespoons

Sift dry ingredients. Cut shortening into flour with 2 knives or pastry blender. Make a hole in center of mixture and put milk into it. Stir until dough comes clean from the sides of the bowl. Knead a few times and dough is ready to be rolled out.

Prune Dumplings

From a recent German immigrant to the Pacific Northwest comes this potato dumpling variation, which uses the Oregon prune in a favorite Old World treat.

Dried prunes 20, pitted
Potatoes 1½ pounds, peeled, cooked, cooled, and sieved
Egg 1
Flour 2 cups
Sugar cubes 20
Water 2 quarts
Salt ½ teaspoon
Butter ½ cup
Bread crumbs ¼ cup
Sugar ¼ cup
Cinnamon 1 teaspoon

Soak prunes until they are plump. Drain well. Mix potatoes, egg, and enough flour to make workable dough. Roll out ½-inch thick on floured board and cut into rounds with biscuit cutter. Put a sugar cube in the center of each prune and wrap dough around it. Simmer water in a 4-quart pot. Add salt. Drop dumplings into simmering water and cook about 10 to 15 minutes until dumplings come to surface of the liquid. Just before serving, melt butter in skillet. Stir in bread crumbs, sugar, and cinnamon. Roll dumplings in the mixture and set on a platter. Makes 20.
Variation: Substitute fresh fruit of any small variety, such as plums or apricots.

Oregon Trail Plum Dumplings

Whole families sought the land of milk and honey at the end of the Oregon Trail in the 1840s. Rather than be left behind, women bravely followed their husbands and found themselves fanning buffalo chip fires to boil beans. "I tried to conceal within my own breast . . . my woes and disappointment . . . ," wrote a diarist. One woman protested her husband's choice of a camping spot and insisted he move farther downstream, away from the pollution of previous travelers. Other wives heard her and got up the courage to protest until their husbands moved to fresh camping spots, too. Sometimes women could coax husbands to stop and pick wild fruit when they saw it along the trail. Prunus Americana, *the wild plum growing east of the Rocky Mountains, would have been used in this dumpling dessert. But no need for you to stop the wagon to pluck plums as canned fruit can be substituted.*

Plums 3 cups pitted
Water 3 cups
Sugar ½ cup or more to taste
Butter 1 tablespoon
Dumplings

Put plums in large kettle with water, sugar, and butter, then simmer until mixture thickens. Drop dumplings into simmering sauce, and simmer slowly, covering pan when dumplings rise to the top, until they are set. Serves 6.

Dumplings

Fine cornmeal ½ cup
Flour ¼ cup
Baking powder ½ teaspoon
Salt ⅛ teaspoon
Brown sugar 2 tablespoons
Butter 2 tablespoons
Egg 1, beaten
Milk ¼ cup

Combine dry ingredients. Cut in butter with 2 knives until mixture is consistency of coarse cornmeal. Stir in egg with a fork, then add milk and mix. Drop by spoonfuls into simmering liquid.

Blackberry Dumplings

Immigrants moved west away from the backbreaking labor of eastern industrial areas as soon as they had means to resettle their families in the wide open spaces. A German woman in this westward migration of the early 1900s found that wild blackberries growing abundantly in her new Oregon home adapted easily to her pinwheel-style dumpling dish.

Flour   2 cups sifted
Baking powder   2 teaspoons
Baking soda   ½ teaspoon
Salt   1 teaspoon
Shortening   ⅓ cup
Buttermilk or sour milk   ⅔ cup
Blackberries   2 cups
Water   2 cups
Sugar   1½ cups

Combine first 4 ingredients in mixing bowl. Cut in shortening with pastry blender or 2 knives until it is broken into fine particles. Add milk and stir with a fork until dough holds together. Gather into a ball, turn onto lightly floured board, and knead gently, about 12 strokes. Roll out dough into a rectangle about ¼-inch thick. Spread berries over dough. Roll up jelly-roll fashion and cut into slices about ½-inch thick. Place cut slices horizontally in the bottom of a 5-quart pot. Pour water and sugar over slices. Cover and let come to a boil. Place on trivet on stove top and simmer until syrup thickens and dough is cooked through. At end of cooking, remove lid and let dumplings dry out a bit more. Serves 8 to 10.

Huckle Buckle

In days past, my friend's aunt Mary would load camping gear and her family into the wagon and drive to the slopes of Oregon's Mount Hood. They would hide the wagon wheels in the brush while they were away from camp picking berries so the wagon would be there when they returned with buckets full of huckleberries. In Portland Town the berries sold at the going rate of five dollars per five-gallon can.

Huckleberries* 2½ cups
Sugar ½ cup
Water 1 cup
Lemon juice 1 tablespoon
Flour 1 cup
Baking powder 1½ teaspoons
Sugar 2 tablespoons
Salt ¼ teaspoon
Butter 1 tablespoon
Milk ½ cup

In a saucepan cook berries, sugar, and water together about 10 minutes. Add lemon juice. Mix together flour, baking powder, sugar, and salt. Cut butter in with pastry blender or 2 knives until mixture resembles coarse cornmeal. Add milk all at once and stir until ingredients are barely mixed. Drop by spoonfuls onto hot huckleberry mixture. When dough rises to top, cover and cook until dough is cooked through. Serves 4.
* Blueberries can be used instead.

Dried Apple Duff

"Seven bells" at half past eleven on an American man-of-war found the ship's cook at mainmast presenting his dinner ration for inspection. *"Serve out,"* ordered the officer of the watch if the dish passed the taste test. A writer in an 1890 Harper's Weekly *pleaded with government powers to train and instruct navy cooks properly just as they did every other officer. He asked for at least one cook in the galley who knew the difference between salt junk (hard salted meat) and dried apple duff. For you who need proper training, the recipe follows.*

Flour 2 cups
Baking powder 2 teaspoons
Salt ½ teaspoon
Sugar ⅔ cup

Butter 1 cup, softened
Dried apple slices 1 cup
Cinnamon ½ teaspoon
Egg 1, beaten
Milk 1 cup
Heavy cream

Sift together first 4 ingredients. Stir in butter. Add remaining ingredients except cream and beat about 3 minutes. Pour into 1½-quart greased mold. Cover tightly with foil, tie with string, and place on a rack in a steamer kettle with 3 inches of simmering water. Cover pot and steam about 3 hours until knife comes out clean. Invert on a dish and serve with cream. Serves 6.

Great Grandma's Carrot Cake

Moist, fruity, and tasty, this cake is the kind that creates legends. June Bradbury Broili of Reno, Nevada, ate the cake as a child just as her mother and grandmother had before her. They started it the day before and baked it in the warm morning oven. Another source says it came across four states in a sheep wagon and stayed moist all the way. Economical and long lasting, it suits today's life-styles just as well.

Sugar 1⅓ cups
Water 1⅓ cups
Raisins 1 cup
Butter ½ cup
Large carrots 2, peeled and finely grated
Cinnamon 1 teaspoon
Nutmeg 1 teaspoon
Nuts 1 cup chopped
Flour 2½ cups sifted
Baking soda 1 teaspoon
Baking powder 2 teaspoons

The night before baking, combine first 7 ingredients in saucepan. Bring to boil on stove top and let sit overnight away from heat. The next morning, place this mixture and the remaining ingredients in a mixing bowl. Stir and pour into lightly greased 5 by 9-inch loaf pan on trivet on stove top. Cover with larger pan. Cook about 2 hours until knife comes out clean. Cool 15 minutes, then remove from pan and cool on rack.
Note: In a conventional oven, bake at 275° for 1 hour and 20 minutes.

Apple Date Dream

Slaves on southern plantations prayed and shouted as readily as they breathed and worked. It was a way of releasing tension and surviving. They always prayed in secret, whether to put their heads in pots, or make knee spots in the canebrakes where they could hide. As they worked, they hummed under their breath to each other, "Steal away, steal away to Jesus." That meant "dere gwine be a 'ligious meetin' dat night... way down in de swamp." When they got there, they shouted all their tensions away. When the sun came up the next day, they were back in the fields or working in the kitchen and big house, the soul of the working plantation. A slave would have been the one who baked this dessert in the kitchens of a Georgia plantation.

Flour   2 cups sifted
Sugar   1 cup
Baking soda   1½ teaspoons
Salt   1 teaspoon
Cinnamon   1 teaspoon
Allspice   ½ teaspoon
Eggs   2, slightly beaten
Stewed apples (see Index)   3 cups
Butter   ½ cup, melted
Vanilla   1 teaspoon
Dates   1 cup chopped
Pecans   ¼ cup chopped
Whipped cream

Sift together flour, sugar, baking soda, salt, cinnamon, and allspice. In a separate bowl, combine eggs, apples, butter, and vanilla. Combine flour mixture and egg mixture and blend well. Stir in dates and pecans. Pour into 2 greased and floured 8-inch round cake pans. Place pans on trivet on stove top and cover each with a larger, inverted cooking pan. Bake 1 hour until knife comes out clean. Cool and serve in wedges with whipped cream. Serves 12.
Note: In a conventional oven, bake at 350° for 25 to 45 minutes.

War Cake

We entered World War I on 6 April 1917, and sent men, supplies, and food across the ocean for the war effort. Herbert Hoover's Food Administration pleaded with people to observe wheatless days, meatless days, and eggless days. Thus restricted, women created cake recipes that were so successful they have survived for our use in today's tight times. This version of war cake was found in kitchen records of the late Sarah Elsie Booth of Oregon's Blue Mountains.

Raisins   2 cups
Molasses   1 cup
Syrup   1 cup
Shortening   ¼ cup
Water   1½ cups
Eggs   2 (optional)*
Rolled oats or cornmeal   ½ cup
Cinnamon   2 teaspoons
Mace or nutmeg   ½ teaspoon
Ground cloves   ½ teaspoon
Ginger   ½ teaspoon
Orange rind   1 tablespoon grated
Whole wheat flour   1 cup
Salt   ¼ teaspoon
Baking soda   1 teaspoon
Baking powder   2½ teaspoons
Syrup   topping
Nuts   garnish, chopped

Boil first 5 ingredients 10 minutes. Add oats and simmer slightly. Cool. Add eggs, if desired, and beat well. Add spices and orange rind. Stir together next 4 ingredients and add to above ingredients. Blend well and pour into greased 1½-quart baking dish or 10-inch tube. Place on trivet on hot stove top. Cover with larger pan and bake about an hour until broom straw comes out clean. Remove from stove, cool, and remove from pan. Brush top with syrup and nuts.
* If the hens laid.
Note: In a conventional oven, bake at 350° for 30 minutes.

Seed Cake

Betsy Patterson, daughter of a Baltimore, Maryland, banker, was swept off her feet by the French naval lieutenant Jerome Bonaparte, whose brother was Napoleon I, self-declared emperor of France. Jerome's ship had taken refuge in New York Harbor while en route to the West Indies in 1803 at the outbreak of war between France and England. Betsy and Jerome were married for three years—long enough for her to write a cookbook and bear a son—before brother Napoleon annulled the marriage and insisted that Jerome remarry into European royalty. Betsy must have vented her feelings while making this cake. The recipe in her book The London Art of Cookery and Housekeeper's Complete Assistant *required beating the batter by hand for two hours.*

Butter 2 cups
Sugar 2¼ cups
Eggs 8, separated
Flour 4 cups
Caraway seeds 6 tablespoons
Grated nutmeg 1 tablespoon
Cinnamon 1 tablespoon

Ingredients should be at room temperature. In a bowl beat butter until it is creamy. Blend in sugar ½ cup at a time, and beat until mixture is thoroughly blended and fluffy. Beat egg whites until stiff, then fold into butter and sugar mixture. Beat egg yolks until they are pale yellow and fold them into mixture. Combine remaining ingredients and fold into batter 1 cup at a time until batter is thoroughly blended and very thick. Spoon into buttered angel cake pan. Set on trivet on stove top and cover with larger pan. Cook about 1½ to 2 hours until knife inserted comes out clean. Immediately remove cake from pan and cool on rack. Texture will be halfway between bread and cake.
Note: In a conventional oven, bake at 375° for no longer than 1½ hours.

Captain's Cake

Captain Amos Adams sailed his good ship Mary Ann *home to Cape Cod one blustery night, but stuck fast on the rocks short of home port. He unshipped his cargo of molasses and coconut, tea and China silk, and a swearing parrot. When he arrived home safely with molasses and coconut, his wife baked him this cake.*

Cake flour 1½ cups sifted
Cream of tartar ½ teaspoon
Baking soda ¼ teaspoon
Salt ½ teaspoon
Sugar ⅓ cup
Butter 3 tablespoons softened
Vanilla 1 teaspoon
Egg yolks 4
Molasses ⅔ cup
Light cream 5 to 6 tablespoons
Coconut 1 cup grated
Maple Cream Frosting

Sift together first 4 ingredients 3 times. Cream sugar and butter. Add vanilla and beat well. Beat egg yolks and add to butter and sugar mixture. Beat until fluffy. Combine flour mixture with butter mixture and beat well. Add molasses and continue beating. Add half of cream, then coconut, then rest of cream. Beat well and spoon into a greased 8-inch square baking pan. Set on trivet on stove top and cover with larger pan. Bake about 30 minutes until knife comes out clean. Cool and ice with frosting.
Note: In a conventional oven, bake at 375° for 35 minutes.

Maple Cream Frosting

Confectioners' sugar 4 cups sifted
Butter or margarine 4 tablespoons
Milk ½ cup
Maple flavoring 1 teaspoon

Beat sugar into butter. Add milk. Stir in flavoring.

Beer Cake

On the floor of a Baltimore brewery, Catherine Pickersgill and her daughter cut and stitched the flag that later flew over Fort McHenry, inspiring Francis Scott Key's poem, "The Star-Spangled Banner." Now our national anthem, it is sung to the tune of an old drinking song. Beer was important as a food to the first Americans, as illustrated by one Mayflower *diarist who wrote on 19 December 1620, "...our victuals being much spent, especially our beer." Besides being a thirst quencher, it was used for leavening, as in this colonial beer cake recipe.*

Dark molasses ½ cup
Butter or oil 2 tablespoons
Egg 1
Dark beer ½ cup
Flour 1¼ cups
Raisins ½ cup
Ginger ¼ teaspoon
Cinnamon ⅛ teaspoon
Cloves ⅛ teaspoon
Nutmeg ⅛ teaspoon
Walnuts ¼ cup chopped
Baking soda 1 teaspoon
Sesame seeds 1 tablespoon

Mix molasses and butter in a large bowl. Add egg and beat well. Add beer alternately with flour. Stir in raisins, spices, and nuts, then add baking soda. Pour into a greased 8-inch square baking pan. Sprinkle with sesame seeds. Set on a trivet and cover with a larger baking pan. Bake until broom straw comes out clean.
Note: In a conventional oven, bake at 350° for 25 minutes.

Booze Cakes

Dubbed "booze" cakes because the liquid used from boiled raisins looks like a brew, this recipe from an eastern Washington State wheat farmer's wife was published in an old farm journal.

Raisins   1 cup
Water   2 cups
Sugar   ¾ cup
Shortening   ½ cup
Egg   1
Vanilla   1 teaspoon
Flour   2 cups
Baking soda   1 teaspoon
Baking powder   2 teaspoons
Cinnamon   ½ teaspoon
Nutmeg   ½ teaspoon
Allspice   ½ teaspoon
Salt   ½ teaspoon
Nuts   ½ cup chopped

Simmer raisins in water until plump and soft. Cream sugar and shortening. Beat in egg. Add vanilla. Sift dry ingredients and stir together with raisins, 1 cup raisin water, and creamed sugar mixture. Fold in nuts. Put batter in greased muffin tins. Set on trivet on stove top and cover with larger baking pan. Cook until broom straw comes out clean. Makes 12.
Note: In a conventional oven, bake at 350° for 25 minutes.

Cheesecake

During World War II, the pursuit of "sugar and spice and all things nice" was curtailed by rationing until cooks realized that since Grandmother had found a way through pioneer life, covered wagons, the Civil War, and World War I to put something sweet on the table, so could they. American Home *magazine introduced this cheesecake in 1943 not only as a sweet but also as a meat substitute.*

Zwieback crumbs 2 cups
Sugar ¼ cup
Cinnamon 1 teaspoon
Butter 3 tablespoons
Eggs 4
Sugar ¾ cup
Salt ¼ teaspoon
Cottage cheese 3 cups
Evaporated milk 1 cup
Flour ¼ cup
Vanilla 1 teaspoon

Mix crumbs, ¼ cup sugar, cinnamon, and butter together. Reserve ½ cup of mixture and line a 9-inch spring-form pan. In a mixing bowl, beat eggs until light, add ¾ cup sugar and salt, and continue beating until fluffy. Add remaining ingredients and beat until smooth. Pour into pan and sprinkle with reserved crumbs. Set on trivet on stove top and cover with larger baking pan. Let cook about an hour until knife comes out clean. Serves 12.
Note: In a conventional oven, bake at 350° for 60 minutes.

Griddle Cookies

The English eat "biscuits" but Americans eat "cookies." They are the same, but we get our term from the Pennsylvania Dutch word koekje *or "little cake." These "little cakes" will evaporate from the stove top when the family gathers around for the evening.*

Flour 3½ cups
Sugar 1 cup
Baking powder 1½ teaspoons
Baking soda ½ teaspoon
Nutmeg ¼ teaspoon
Shortening 1 cup
Egg 1, beaten
Milk ½ cup
Lemon zest 1 tablespoon

Sift dry ingredients. Cut in shortening with pastry blender or 2 knives. Combine egg and milk with zest, then add to mixture. Roll out to ⅛-inch thickness and cut with round cutter. Heat oiled griddle on stove top until water dances. Place cookies on griddle. As bottoms brown, tops will puff. Turn and brown other side. Serve hot. Makes 24.

Pineapple Nugget Cookies

A sixteen-year-old girl brought this cookie recipe with her from Ireland to Boston and her granddaughter shares it with us. Butterscotch bits were added as a modern convenience, but the pineapple made the cookie unique. Pineapple has been enjoyed the world over since it was discovered in tropical South America by Spanish explorers. King Charles II of England served it to his guests and other Englishmen grew it as an exotic in their private gardens before it came to colonial America.

Flour 1 cup
Baking powder ½ teaspoon
Salt ¼ teaspoon (optional)
Shortening ¼ cup
Brown sugar ¼ cup
Granulated sugar ¼ cup
Egg 1
Vanilla ½ teaspoon
Butterscotch bits 3 ounces
Crushed pineapple 8-ounce can, well drained

Sift together flour, baking powder, and salt (if desired). Cream shortening, gradually add sugars, and beat until light. Add egg and vanilla and beat well. Add dry ingredients and mix until smooth. Stir in butterscotch and pineapple. Spread in greased 8-inch square pan. Set on trivet on stove top and cover with larger baking pan. Bake until broom straw comes out clean. Remove from heat and cut into 16 bars. Makes 16.
Note: In a conventional oven, bake at 350° for 20 minutes.

Brown Sugar Shortbread

After the Enterprise *made the first steamboat journey upstream from New Orleans to Louisville, Kentucky, in 1815, life changed dramatically for Kentucky backwoods homemakers. When Louisville boatmen hauled goods down to New Orleans on the downstream currents, they dismantled their Kentucky broadhorns (flatboats) and sold the heavy timbers and plankings as building materials and fuel. As they walked back home over the Natchez Trace, they were not likely to bring home a bag of Louisiana sugar—or any other household goods. Everything had to come downstream from the north or overland from the east. So housewives sweetened baked goods with brown maple sugar, "long sweetening" (coarse sorghum), or honey. Recipes like this one from the Locust Grove, home of George Rogers Clark in Louisville, used brown sugar—and very little of it.*

Butter ½ cup
Brown sugar ½ cup
Egg 1, unbeaten
Flour 2 cups sifted

Cream butter and sugar in a bowl until light. Add egg and mix well. Blend in flour and knead dough until smooth. Press dough into a 9-inch iron skillet. Cut the dough into wedges by piercing lines with the tines of a fork. Place skillet on trivet on stove top. Cover with larger, inverted baking pan. Cook about 30 to 45 minutes until shortbread is done through.
Note: In a conventional oven, bake at 400° about 15 minutes until light brown.

Tea Cookies

Muskegon, Michigan, was the "Lumber Queen of the World." One would guess it was the town where loggers had more fun since it was mentioned in more logging ballads than any other town or city. When a cow allegedly kicked over a lantern 8 October 1871, a thriving, new Chicago, 100 miles down Lake Michigan, burned to the ground. Some 90,000 people immediately needed lumber for new homes. That lumber came from Muskegon—much of it from the mills of Charles Henry Hackley, lumberman and benefactor. Mrs. Hackley, in her large Victorian home built in 1880—indoor plumbing included—had her wood hauled up from the basement on a dumbwaiter when she was ready to bake these cookies.

Butter 1 cup, melted
Flour 4 cups
Baking soda 1 teaspoon
Eggs 3, beaten
Brown sugar 2 cups
Ginger ½ teaspoon

Mix together butter, flour, and soda. Beat eggs together with brown sugar and ginger. Combine egg mixture with flour mixture. Drop on greased cast-iron skillet placed on trivet on stove top. Press dough flat with bottom of glass. Cover skillet with inverted roasting pan. Bake cookies 8 to 10 minutes or until center bounces back when touched. Makes 4 dozen.
Note: In a conventional oven, bake at 375° for 10 to 12 minutes.

Taffy Creams

On one expedition to the South Pole, Admiral Richard E. Byrd took 100 pounds of candy for each man in his party. That was two and a half tons of candy! If he had taken this old recipe, his men could have passed long evenings aboard ship pulling taffy.

Water ½ cup
Sugar 2 cups
Salt ¼ teaspoon
Baking soda ⅛ teaspoon
Heavy cream ½ cup
Peppermint flavoring ½ teaspoon
Vanilla ½ teaspoon

Butter and chill 3 cookie sheets. Combine first 4 ingredients in saucepan. Cook and stir until syrup reaches 250°F and spins a 3-inch thread. Add cream 1 tablespoon at a time so boiling does not stop. Cook to thread stage again. Remove from stove and stir in flavorings. Pour in thin ribbons on cookie sheets, then let stand 5 minutes. Pick up ribbons and pull until they are a pale ivory color and taffylike. Cut into 1½-inch lengths. Store in airtight container.

Peanut Butter Candy

At her Elba, Arkansas, boarding house by the Missouri and North Arkansas Railroad line, Arminta Kuykendoll Treat Buchanan made this candy on top of her wood stove in a cast-iron "spider." That was in 1873 when peanuts were being rediscovered and transients found Arminta's candy a treat worth spending an extra night to taste.

Sugar 2 cups
Milk ¾ cup
Vanilla 1 teaspoon
Peanut butter ¼ cup

Bring sugar and milk to boil in an iron skillet (a "spider"). Cook until mixture reaches 238°F and forms a soft ball when a small amount is dropped into cold water. Remove from heat. Add vanilla and peanut butter and beat until creamy. Pour onto buttered platter and cool, then cut into 1-inch squares.

Date Candy

This "spider" candy recipe, found written in blurred ink on the flyleaf of an old cookbook, was to be cooked in a three-legged iron skillet that stood over hot coals of an open hearth.

Sugar 2 cups
Milk ¾ cup
Butter size of a walnut (2 tablespoons)
Dates 1 cup chopped
Nuts 1 cup chopped

Combine sugar, milk, and butter in an iron skillet and cook to soft ball stage (238°F). Add dates and simmer 7 minutes. Remove from stove, add nuts, and beat until stiff. Form into roll and cool, wrapped in damp dish towel. Then slice.

Rhubarb Conserve

Seattle is a city that moves when it needs to. Its founders first settled on Alki Point in 1851, but quickly moved around Puget Sound to Elliott Bay when they discovered the harbor wasn't deep enough. When a glue pot overturned in a woodworking shop and burned down the business district in 1889, the city fathers quickly met and made plans to rebuild an even better city. With this same spirit of improvement, the city reacted to skyrocketing farm-

produce prices in 1907 by passing an ordinance that would allow the consumer to deal directly with the farmer instead of going through greedy middlemen. Pike Place Market—an experimental farmers' market—opened Saturday, 17 August 1907 when H.O. Blanchard arrived from Renton Junction with a load of produce in his wagon for a cheering, waiting crowd. Within the hour, his produce was sold out, as was that of other farmers who had followed. Rhubarb, also known as pieplant, was one of the first vegetables—right, it's not a fruit—these farmers brought in the spring and one of the last they continued to sell in the fall. It is still bountiful at the Pike Place Market.

Rhubarb   4 cups finely chopped
Sugar   6 cups
Lemon   1, juice and grated rind
Orange   1, juice and grated rind
Almonds   1 cup blanched and sliced

Mix rhubarb, sugar, lemon juice and rind, and orange juice and rind in a 4-quart cooking pot. Cover and set on a trivet on stove top to cook until sugar is melted and mixture boils down, about 2 hours. Stir occasionally. Stir in almonds and cook about 10 to 20 minutes more. Store in 1-quart, sterilized canning jar.

Appalachian Apple Butter

Apple butter was traditionally cooked in large cast-iron pots over open fires in the Appalachian Mountains. Cooking this condiment over wood heat gives it the color and flavor reminiscent of an Indian-summer day in the green wooded mountain valleys.

Apples   10 quarts, cored, peeled, and quartered
Water
Sweet cider   2 quarts
Sugar   6 cups
Cinnamon   1 tablespoon
Cloves   1½ teaspoons
Allspice   dash

Place apples in a large cast-iron kettle with only enough water to prevent scorching. Cook about 6 hours until it turns to a paste. Add remaining ingredients and simmer slowly on back of stove 6 to 8 hours or until no liquid runs from apple butter when a spoonful is poured on a cold plate. Add cider to thin butter if you overcook it. Put in sterilized jars and seal. Makes 5 quarts.

Stove-Top Parties

Entertain around the wood stove and you'll feel like a guest at your own party. You can cook on the stove and serve straight from the cooking pots. For large parties, cook ahead and reheat before guests arrive. This collection of ethnic party menus and recipes (asterisks indicate recipes included in the following pages) provides a festive cultural experience worth sharing with your friends.

Finnish Wood Gathering Party

   Finnish woodmen were the folk who cleared the forests to build Philadelphia and taught English settlers to build log cabins with horizontal logs rather than in the upright stockade style. Later, tens of thousands of Finnish immigrants settled in Minnesota, Wisconsin, and Michigan to clear land for cities and highways.
   After wood gathering with friends, spread a buffet like the Finns. Fill bread and butter plates with one course at a time, served in the order below for proper Finnish etiquette. It works well as a potluck, so give your friends the recipes to cook ahead and bring on wood day. Reheat the dishes on top of the stove when it is time to eat. Furnish each guest with a large blue and white checkered napkin and the bread and butter plate. You may change plates after the fish course and proceed to dessert and coffee. Serves 8.

Pickled Herring

Pork Roast*

Potato Casserole*   Sliced Tomatoes

Hot Squash Salad*

Pulla Coffee Bread*

Kermakakku*   Viikunakakku
(Sour Cream Cake)   (Fig Butter Cake)

Coffee

Pork Roast*

Molasses 1 cup
Salt 2 tablespoons
Peppercorns 1 tablespoon crushed
Allspice 1 tablespoon
Pork roast 6 pounds
Prepared mustard 3 tablespoons
Cinnamon 1 teaspoon
Whole cloves 20
Bread crumbs 1 cup
Water

Combine first 4 ingredients and rub over roast. Put in a large bowl and refrigerate 3 to 4 days. Spoon juices over meat several times a day. Remove from bowl and dry with towel. On the day you want to serve the roast, mix mustard and cinnamon and rub on roast. Stud meat with cloves and sprinkle with crumbs. Place meat on a small rack inside a Dutch oven and put a small amount of water in the bottom. Set on stove top and bake several hours until roast tests done.
* This must be started several days ahead.
Note: On conventional stove, cook at 325° for 3½ hours.

Potato Casserole

Potatoes 2 pounds scrubbed
Butter 2 tablespoons
Flour 2 tablespoons
Milk 2 cups
Salt 1 teaspoon

The night before serving, boil potatoes until done. While still hot, peel and mash them in a large bowl with butter. Add 1 tablespoon flour and mix well. Cover bowl and let stand in a warm place overnight. The next day, add remaining 1 tablespoon flour and mix well. Add milk, stir in salt, and blend well. Pour mixture into a greased 3-quart casserole. Set on trivet on stove top, cover, and cook several hours until potatoes are tender and milk is thickened.
Note: In a conventional oven, cook at 300° for 3 hours.

Hot Squash Salad

Sugar 1 cup
White wine vinegar ½ cup
Water 1 cup
Winter squash 4 cups cubed
Whole cloves 3

Combine sugar, vinegar, and water. Pour over squash in a large kettle with a lid. Add cloves, cover, and simmer on stove top on a trivet until squash is tender. Serve hot from stove top. Serves 8.

Pulla Coffee Bread

Active dry yeast   2 teaspoons
Warm water   ½ cup
Milk   2 cups, scalded and cooled to lukewarm
Sugar   1 cup
Salt   1 teaspoon
Cardamom   1 teaspoon
Eggs   4, beaten
Flour   8 to 9 cups sifted
Butter   ½ cup, melted
Glaze

Dissolve yeast in warm water. Stir in next 5 ingredients and 2 cups flour. Beat until dough is smooth and elastic. Add 3 cups flour and beat well. Add butter and stir well. Beat until dough looks glossy and stir in remaining flour to form stiff dough. Rest dough on floured board about 15 minutes, then knead until smooth. Place in greased mixing bowl and turn to grease top. Cover and let rise about 1 hour until doubled in bulk. Punch down. Let rise about 30 minutes until doubled again. Turn out onto floured board. Divide into 3 parts. Divide those parts into 3. Form dough into a 16-inch long strip, rolling between palms and the board. Braid 3 strips together and pinch ends, then tuck under. Keep remaining dough in refrigerator until ready to bake. Place on lightly greased baking sheet and let rise 20 minutes. Place baking sheet on trivets and glaze loaf. Cover baking pan with large roasting pan. Cook on stove top until loaf sounds hollow when thumped. Makes 3 braids.
Note: In a conventional oven, bake at 400° for 25 minutes.

Glaze

Egg   1, beaten
Sugar cubes   ½ cup crushed
Almonds   ½ cup sliced

Brush egg onto braids and sprinkle with sugar and almonds.

Kermakakku   (Sour Cream Cake)

Egg   1, beaten
Sour cream   1 cup
Granulated sugar   1 cup
Almond extract   1 or 2 drops
Flour   1½ cups
Baking soda   ½ teaspoon
Salt   ¼ teaspoon
Cinnamon   ¼ teaspoon
Cardamom   ⅛ teaspoon
Granulated sugar

Combine first 4 ingredients in a mixing bowl. Sift together remaining ingredients except sugar for dusting. Gradually add dry mixture to egg mixture, beating until smooth. Grease a 5 by 9-inch loaf pan and dust with sugar. Set on trivet on stove top and cover with roasting pan. Bake about an hour until broom straw comes out clean. Cool, then remove from pan. Makes 1 loaf.
Note: In a conventional oven, bake at 350° for 40 minutes.

Viikunakakku   (Fig Butter Cake)

Butter   ¾ cup
Sugar   ¾ cup
Eggs   3, beaten
Orange zest   2 tablespoons
Flour   1½ cups sifted
Baking powder   1 teaspoon
Dried figs   ½ cup chopped
Raisins   ½ cup
Walnuts   ¼ cup chopped
Ground almonds or sugar
Confectioners' sugar

Cream butter and sugar until lemon colored. Add eggs and orange zest. Sift flour with baking powder. Remove 2 tablespoons and combine with figs, raisins, and nuts. Gradually add remaining flour to creamed mixture. Beat until smooth. Stir in fruit-nut mix. Grease a 5 by 9-inch loaf pan well and dust with almonds. Set on trivet on stove top and cover with inverted larger baking pan. Cook about an hour until broom straw comes out clean. Dust with sugar and slice into thin pieces. Makes 1 loaf.
Note: In a conventional oven, bake at 350° for 45 minutes.

Southern Cocktail Party

Tennessee frontier party fare of sorghum and molasses treats with corn bread has been replaced by these classic dishes served on silver platters. The plainest foods become sophisticated when served with style and Southern hospitality.

These cocktail appetizers come from Nashville—home of President Andrew Jackson, who rose from a lowly birth in a log cabin to preside at the White House. He gave the common man hopes and dreams because of his own life and his slogan "Let the People Rule."

Just plain folks will feel like royalty when you hold this party. Put the dishes in attractive heat-proof serving ware—pewter, stainless, Pyrex, or silver—on trivets atop the stove. Give each guest a small cocktail napkin, a china plate large enough to hold small portions of food, and a crystal glass. Then introduce them to the stove top to help themselves. Serves 40.

Hot Clam Dip*

Deviled Crab*   Mushrooms Divine*

Eggplant Appetizer*

Hot Tangy Tomato Juice*

Apricot Fondue*

Coffee*

Mixed Drinks

Hot Clam Dip

Clams   two 7-ounce cans minced
Cream cheese   three 8-ounce packages
Clam juice
Lemon juice   3 tablespoons
Medium onion   ½, minced
Worcestershire sauce   1½ tablespoons
Cayenne   to taste
Salt   to taste
Melba toast rounds

Mix all ingredients together in a heat-proof dish. Place on trivet on stove top over warm spot and heat through. Serve with toast rounds.

Deviled Crab

Crab   6 cups boiled and picked, reserving shell
Bread crumbs   ¾ cup
Dry mustard   ¾ teaspoon
Nutmeg   ¾ teaspoon
Mace   ¾ teaspoon
Ground cloves   ⅛ teaspoon
Butter   3 tablespoons, melted
Egg yolks   3, beaten
Worcestershire sauce   ⅛ teaspoon
Sherry   1½ cups

Combine crab with all remaining ingredients. Scrub crab shell and fill with combined mixture. Place filled shells on heat-proof serving dish. Set on stove top over trivet, cover dish, and heat through. Serve from stove top with small serving forks.

Mushrooms Divine

Fresh whole mushrooms   6 cups
Red-hot pork sausage   3 pounds

Wash and scrub mushrooms. Remove stems, chop them finely into sausage, and mix well. Stuff mushrooms and place in baking pan on trivet on stove top. Cover dish and cook until sausage is done. Serve from stove top on trivet.

Eggplant Appetizer

Olive or salad oil ½ cup plus 2 tablespoons
Large eggplant 1, cut into ½-inch pieces
Onions 2½ cups sliced
Celery 1 cup diced
Tomato sauce two 15-ounce cans
Red wine vinegar ¼ cup
Sugar 2 teaspoons
Capers 2 tablespoons drained
Salt ½ teaspoon
Pepper dash
Black olives 12, pitted and sliced
Whole wheat crackers

Heat oil in skillet and sauté eggplant. Remove from pan and add onions and celery to skillet. Return eggplant and add tomato sauce. Simmer 15 minutes. Add remaining ingredients and simmer 30 minutes. Remove from heat and refrigerate overnight. Serve with crackers.

Hot Tangy Tomato Juice

Tomato juice 46-ounce can
Consommé (see Index) 1½ quarts
Water 1½ quarts
Worcestershire sauce 2 tablespoons
Salt 1 teaspoon
Bay leaf 1

Combine all ingredients in an attractive kettle. Simmer about 5 minutes. Put on trivet on stove top and serve hot. Remove bay leaf before serving.

Apricot Fondue

Apricot halves   four 30-ounce cans, unpeeled, drained
Sugar   1⅓ cups
Cornstarch   4 tablespoons
Whipping cream   3 cups
Lemon juice   4 tablespoons
Fresh pears   5 cups cut in chunks
Angel cake   5 cups cut in chunks

Puree apricots until smooth. In a fondue pot combine sugar and cornstarch. Stir in apricot puree, cream, and lemon juice. Set pot on stove and stir until thickened, bubbly, and somewhat caramelized. To serve, set on trivet on stove top. With toothpicks, spear chunks of pear and angel cake for dipping in fondue.

Coffee

Egg   1, plus shell
Regular grind coffee   1¼ pounds
Cold water   1 cup
Water   9 quarts

Mix egg, shell and all, with coffee. Add cold water. Tie mixture in a large cheesecloth bag. Immerse bag in large pot with remaining water. Bring to a boil. Move to low heat part of stove for about 5 minutes. Remove coffee bag. Keep hot on stove top.

Tex-Mex Barbecue

Mexicans became Texans when the state severed itself from Mexico in 1836 after the Mexicans' victory at Fort Alamo and the retaliation by Sam Houston at the Battle of San Jacinto. At this party, hot spicy beans share the same plate with barbecued Texas beef. The French buccaneers who explored the region in 1685 left behind the word barbecue, *which means to skewer a whole animal—from the whiskers* (barbe) *to the tail* (queue)— *then cook it.*

From the Rio Grande valley along the now Mexican border, these Tex-Mex recipes honorably unite the two peoples. Serve up extra flair with bold linens of red, green, and white, and use earthenware dishes and a tasseled tissue piñata for a centerpiece. Serves 8.

Queso*

Barbecued Short Ribs*

or Barbecued Chicken*

Salsa Jalapeño*   Guacamole

Tamales*   Frijoles Refritos*

Pralines*

Limeade with Mint Leaves

Queso

Mozzarella, Monterey Jack, or Havarti cheese   1 pound, grated
Vegetable oil   3 tablespoons
Large onion   1, chopped
Bell pepper   ½ cup chopped
Mushrooms   1 pound, sliced
Whipping cream   ½ cup
Flour tortillas   18 to 20, warmed

In a shallow casserole, spread cheese evenly and place on stove top until cheese softens. In a large skillet, heat oil and sauté onion and bell pepper until onion is soft. Stir in mushrooms and continue stirring until mushrooms begin to darken. Stir cream into cheese, mixing well.

Gradually stir in mushroom mixture. When thoroughly blended, spoon over tortillas. Serve as appetizer or main dish.

Barbecued Short Ribs

Beef short ribs 8 pounds
Catsup 1 cup
Molasses ½ cup
Lemon juice ½ cup
Dry mustard 1½ tablespoons
Chili powder ½ teaspoon
Worcestershire sauce 3 tablespoons
Celery ½ cup chopped
Salt 1 teaspoon
Water ½ cup

Place Dutch oven on stove top to heat. Trim excess fat from ribs and put in Dutch oven. Brown ribs on both sides. Combine remaining ingredients and pour over browned ribs. Cover pot and cook several hours, basting or turning ribs occasionally until meat begins to pull away from the bone.

Barbecued Chicken

Chickens 2, 3½ pounds each, split
Lemon juice 2 tablespoons
Garlic cloves 4, minced
Coarse salt ¼ cup
Sweet Hungarian paprika 2 tablespoons
Ground red pepper 2 teaspoons

Pat chicken dry and rub with lemon juice and garlic. Combine remaining ingredients and sprinkle over chicken. Refrigerate overnight on a rack over a baking pan. To cook, if your stove has burner holes, remove a lid and place the rack of chicken over the open hole and roast on each side about 20 to 30 minutes. Otherwise, cook chicken covered in a Dutch oven, turning once during cooking until chicken begins to pull away from the bone.

Salsa Jalapeño

Jalapeño peppers 20
Stewed tomatoes 14½-ounce can
Salt ½ teaspoon
Garlic clove 1, minced
Small onion ½, chopped
Tomato sauce 8-ounce can

Toast peppers in a dry frying pan until skin is burned, then put them in a wet towel and let steam for about 20 minutes. Pull off skin and mash them with an empty glass. Combine with all other ingredients. Let simmer about 30 minutes until everything is cooked through and blended. Serve over tamales, beans, and meat. Makes about 1 quart.

Tamales

Shortening 2 cups
Masa harina 8 cups
Warm Chicken Stock (see Index) 3 cups
Baking powder 2 tablespoons
Salt 1 tablespoon
Yellow corn husks 36, dried or green
Picadillo
Salsa Jalapeño (optional)

In large mixing bowl, beat shortening until fluffy. Gradually add masa harina, alternating with stock (be sure it is not too warm). Stir in baking powder and salt. Soak husks overnight in cold water. Drain and dry with towels. Spread dough on husks, with a 1-inch border down the long side. Spoon 1 or 2 tablespoons Picadillo down center of dough. Fold husk in half lengthwise. Fold again, joining narrow halves to make packets, open at 1 end. Place tamales open ends upright in a steamer kettle with 1 inch of water. Place on stove top and let steam a couple of hours. Serve with Salsa Jalapeño if desired.

Picadillo

Vegetable oil 2 tablespoons
Medium onion 1, chopped
Lean ground beef 1½ pounds
Tomatoes 16-ounce can
Tomato paste 6-ounce can

Raisins   ½ cup
Vinegar   2 tablespoons
Chili powder   1 tablespoon
Cinnamon   1 teaspoon
Ground cumin   1 teaspoon
Sugar   1 teaspoon
Cloves   pinch
Mushrooms   2 cups sliced
Almonds   ½ cup toasted and chopped
Jalapeno peppers   2 or 3, seeded and finely chopped

Heat oil in large saucepan. Add onion and sauté. Add beef and brown. Add next 9 ingredients and simmer about an hour until they are well blended. Stir in mushrooms and continue to simmer about 30 minutes. Stir in almonds and peppers. Freezes well. Makes about 6 cups.
Note: This filling also is good in tacos and chiles rellenos.

Frijoles Refritos

Dried small red beans   ½ pound
Water   5 cups
Onion   ¼ cup chopped
Bacon drippings   1 tablespoon
Salt   1½ teaspoons
Bacon drippings   5 tablespoons
Onion   ¼ cup finely minced
Lettuce   shredded
Mozzarella cheese   grated

Soak beans in water overnight, then cook about 2 hours until tender. Add onion and 1 tablespoon drippings and continue to simmer about 30 minutes. Add salt. In a large skillet, heat 5 tablespoons drippings. Cook remaining onion in drippings until soft. Add 1 cup beans and some of their cooking liquid. Mash well with a wooden mallet. Continue adding beans and liquid and mashing until mixture is pasty. Cook and stir beans until mixture dries out and beans come away from skillet. Garnish with lettuce and cheese.

Pralines

Sugar 3 cups
Buttermilk 1½ cups
Baking soda ½ teaspoon
Butter 2 tablespoons
Pecan halves 2 cups
Vanilla 2 teaspoons

Combine sugar, buttermilk, and baking soda in heavy pan and stir. Let mixture come to a boil and simmer gently until syrup reaches a soft ball stage (238 °F) when dropped into a cup of cold water. Remove from heat. Add butter and beat with wooden spoon until mixture is dull looking. Stir in nuts and vanilla. Work quickly. Drop spoonfuls onto baking sheets covered with waxed paper.

Basque Boardinghouse Spread

Tucked between Spain and France from the Bay of Biscay to the Pyrenees Mountains, the Basque people enjoyed a paradise of shady lanes and sun-soaked vineyards. When politics and economics squeezed them out of their homeland, these spirited seafaring people turned to America, where they herded sheep in the lonely, barren ranges of California, Nevada, and Idaho. Today, the Boise Valley has the largest concentration in the world of Basques outside their homeland.

Boardinghouses provided homes for the many single men who came into towns to shear and ship the sheep. The Rumirez family came to the southeastern Oregon town of Burns in 1925 and built a twenty-room boardinghouse. These favorite dishes from the Basques of Burns and Boise spread a boardinghouse table.

Cook and serve right from the stove top. Use white bone china on Basque flag colors of red and green linen, with accordian music and fresh flowers. Serves 8.

Bacalado-con-Pimiento*
(Codfish with Pimientos)

La Garbure*   Lengua-con-Setas*
(Stew)   (Tongue with Mushroom Sauce)

Arrosa Chirlagas eta Peregilgas*
(Rice and Clams)

Pears in Red Wine*   Flana*

Sheepherder's Bread*
or French Sourdough Bread

Red Wine

Bacalado-con-Pimiento (Codfish with Pimientos)

Salted codfish 1 package
Water
Flour
Egg 1, beaten
Vegetable oil 1 tablespoon
Garlic clove 1, minced
Pimientos 4-ounce jar, cut in strips or
    Fresh pimiento 1, cut in strips

Soak fish in water overnight, changing water at least twice. Remove fish from water, pat dry, and cut into chunks. Dip in flour and then in egg. Heat oil in wide flat skillet with lid. Put garlic and fish into oil and fry, first on 1 side and then on the other, until golden brown. Put pimiento on top of fish. Cover pan and place on trivet on stove top. Cook about an hour.
Note: In a conventional oven, cook at 300° for 1 hour.

La Garbure (Stew)

Bulk bacon ½ pound
Water 4 quarts
Potatoes 2 cups peeled and cubed
Leeks 6, sliced
Turnips 4, cut in chunks
Onions 1½ cups chopped
Carrots 5, peeled and sliced
Peas 2 cups
Lima beans 2 cups
Salt 1 tablespoon or to taste
Chorizo* ¾ pound peeled
Small cabbage 1, sliced
Green peppers 2, chopped

Put bacon and water in a heavy pan and bring to a boil. Add next 7 ingredients and bring to a simmer. Add salt and let simmer until vegetables are tender. Add sausage, cabbage, and peppers. Simmer until mixture thickens and vegetables are soft. Remove bacon from pot and slice before returning to pot. Adjust salt to taste.
* Spanish-style sausage.

Lengua-con-Setas (Tongue with Mushroom Sauce)

Beef tongue 1, boiled until tender and skinned
Flour
Eggs 2, beaten
Vegetable oil ½ cup
Onion 1, chopped
Tomato juice 1 cup
Flour ¼ cup
Butter or margarine ¼ cup, melted
Milk 1 cup
Mushrooms 1 cup chopped
Salt and pepper to taste

Slice tongue and dip in flour and then in eggs. Heat oil in skillet and brown slices of battered tongue on 1 side. Add onion to pan and turn tongue to other side. Cook until onions are soft. Mix next 5 ingredients together and pour over meat. Place on trivet on stove top and cover skillet. Cook at least an hour before serving from stove top.

Arrosa Chirlagas eta Peregilgas (Rice and Clams)

Vegetable oil
Medium onion 1, chopped
Green pepper 1, diced
Pimiento 4-ounce jar or
    Fresh pimiento 1, cut in strips
Rice 1 cup uncooked
Clams 10-ounce can, chopped
Tomato sauce ½ cup
Peas ½ cup
Hot water 2 quarts
Parsley ¼ cup chopped
Salt and pepper to taste

Heat oil in large saucepan. Sauté onion, green pepper, and pimiento. Stir in rice and brown slightly. Add next 5 ingredients, then add salt and pepper. Cover tightly and cook on stove top until rice is tender.

Pears in Red Wine

Firm, ripe fall pears   6, peeled
Red wine   1 cup
Honey   1 cup
Cinnamon stick   one, 1 inch
Cloves   ¼ teaspoon
Lemon peel   1-inch piece
Warm milk or cold custard sauce   topping

Cut pears in half and core. Combine remaining ingredients and simmer in saucepan. Add pears to syrup and cook until they are soft but still firm. Discard cinnamon stick and lemon peel. Serve with milk.

Flana

Eggs   4
Sugar   ½ cup
Salt   pinch
Milk   2 cups
Vanilla   1 teaspoon
Sugar   ½ cup

Beat eggs slightly in a bowl and stir in ½ cup sugar and salt. Scald milk in a saucepan, then stir slowly into egg mixture. Add vanilla. Pour ½ cup sugar in a 1-quart custard pan and put on stove top to melt until it is a brown liquid. Add a bit of water if necessary. Pour in egg and milk mixture. Set pan on a rack in steamer kettle with 2 inches of hot water. Cover kettle, put on stove top, and cook until custard is firm and knife comes out clean. When ready to serve, invert custard on a platter.

Sheepherder's Bread

Hot water   1½ cups
Butter or margarine   ¼ cup
Sugar   ¼ cup
Salt   1¼ teaspoons
Active dry yeast   2 ounces
Flour   5 cups
Oil

Combine first 4 ingredients in a large bowl. Stir and cool to 110°. Stir in yeast and set aside until yeast is bubbly. Add half the flour and beat well. Stir in remaining flour until dough pulls away from sides of bowl. Turn dough onto a floured board and knead about 10 minutes until dough becomes elastic. Place in a greased bowl and turn once. Let rise about 1½ hours until double. Punch down dough and knead again. Oil the inside of a heavy pot and the inside of the lid. Put dough in pot and let rise about 1 hour. Put lid on pot and place pot atop a trivet on stove top. Bake until loaf sounds hollow when thumped. Serve without butter.
Note: In a conventional oven, bake at 375° for 12 minutes, then put lid on and bake 30 more minutes.

Pueblo-Navajo Feast

Indians of the southwestern United States created this traditional feast with foods native to America—squash, pumpkin, beans, and peppers—and new foods brought by white men—pork, apricots, and rice. For them, food was a precious gift given by the Great Spirit and was to be treated reverently and praised with dance. A little of the gift was to be returned in thanks at each meal by throwing bits to the spirit of fire or earth. As the Indians would, serve these dishes with reverence to the spirits of sun, rain, and wind, who nourish you with these gifts. Use a homespun cotton tablecloth, pottery dishes, and a centerpiece of dried Indian corn. Serves 8.

Summer Squash Soup*

Feast Day Pork Roast*

Succotash*   Corn-Pumpkin Bread*

Hot Chili Sauce

Apricot-Rice Pudding*

Summer Squash Soup

Butter ¾ cup
Medium yellow summer squash 8, cubed
Garlic cloves 2, minced
Green onions 6, chopped
Chili powder 2 teaspoons
Fresh dill 2 tablespoons chopped
Chicken Stock (see Index) 3 cups
Milk 1 cup

Melt butter in saucepan and sauté next 5 ingredients. Smash squash with a potato masher, stirring in stock as you mash. When it is smooth and well blended, add milk and heat through to serve.

Feast Day Pork Roast

Garlic clove 1, minced
Dried sage 1 teaspoon
Dried oregano 1 teaspoon
Salt 2 teaspoons
Pork roast 4 pounds
Onion 1 tablespoon chopped
Green pepper ½ cup chopped
Flour ⅓ cup
Chili powder 1 teaspoon
Tomato puree 2 cups
Raisins ½ cup

Combine first 4 ingredients and rub into roast. Put roast fat side up in roasting pan. Set on trivet on stove top and cook several hours until meat thermometer registers 185°F. Remove roast from pan and set aside. Keeping pan directly on stove top, add onion and green pepper to drippings in pan and sauté until soft. Combine remaining ingredients and add to skillet. Simmer about 10 minutes until sauce thickens. Return roast to pan and baste with sauce. Cover pan and let roast cook another 20 minutes, basting several times.

Succotash

Dried pinto beans 1½ cups
Water
Corn 1½ cups
Green beans 1½ cups chopped
Water 1½ cups
Butter 2 tablespoons
Sugar 1 teaspoon
Salt 1 teaspoon or to taste
Pepper to taste
Butter 2 tablespoons
Sunflower seeds 2 teaspoons crushed

Cover pinto beans with water and soak several hours. Place on stove in saucepan and cook until tender. Drain off excess water and combine beans in heavy saucepan with next 7 ingredients. Cover and place on low heat spot. Simmer until all vegetables are tender. Add 2 tablespoons butter and seeds and simmer until liquid has thickened.

Corn-Pumpkin Bread

Coarse cornmeal 1½ cups
Salt 1 teaspoon
Baking powder 2 teaspoons
Baking soda ¼ teaspoon
Pumpkin 1 cup pureed
Buttermilk ½ cup
Egg 1
Shortening 2 tablespoons melted

Mix together first 4 ingredients. Stir in pumpkin and gradually add milk, egg, and shortening. Heat a well-greased Dutch oven on stove top. Put dough into Dutch oven, cover, and place on stove top. Use trivet if necessary to prevent burning. Cook until bread sounds hollow when tapped.

Apricot-Rice Pudding

Dried apricots ⅓ cup
Rice 3 tablespoons uncooked
Sugar 1 tablespoon
Milk 4 cups
Salt ¼ teaspoon
Cinnamon ¾ teaspoon
Eggs 2

Soak apricots until soft and dice. Combine everything except eggs. Separate eggs, then beat whites until stiff. Beat yolks and gently fold into whites. Fold egg mixture into rice mixture. Pour into a greased 1½-quart casserole. Cover, place on rack in steamer kettle, and add a couple of inches of water. Cover kettle and let cook a couple of hours, stirring mixture occasionally, until rice is tender.

Welsh Tea

Welsh immigrants left their land of mountains and deep green valleys in the early nineteenth century and brought their songs, language, and religion to the United States, hoping to keep all things Welsh intact. They lost most of them to Americanism, but their singing survived. Church and community song fests remain the greatest recreation of Welsh descendants in this country.

Hold a Welsh tea on a Sunday afternoon with your singing friends. Savories, sweets, and strong tea that kept the working man's soul in harmony make this a gala Welsh tea stove top party, which will bring out the Welsh in all of us. Serve the fare with handwoven linens and ironstone cups and plates in a green and white color scheme. A true Welshman would display the ancient druid red dragon with an upright knotted tail and fill the air with harp music. Serves 10.

Strong Tea*

Teisen Cymraeg*   Barabrith*
(Welsh Cakes)   (Raisin Bread)

Seed Cake (See Index)

Selsig Mor Gannug*
(Glamorgan Sausages)

Lemon Curd* and Toast

Butter   Cheese   Orange Marmalade

Salmon Spread

Strong Tea

Water 2 quarts
Tea bags 4
Milk to taste
Sugar to taste

Boil water and pour over tea bags in teapot. Set pot on a trivet on the back of the stove to steep 15 to 30 minutes or all day as the Welsh do. Pour into cups and let guests add their own milk and sugar.

Teisen Cymraeg   (Welsh Cakes)

Flour   3 cups
Baking powder   3 teaspoons
Salt   ½ teaspoon
Butter   ¾ cup
Currants   1 cup
Sugar   ½ cup
Egg   1
Milk   3 to 4 tablespoons
Granulated sugar   1 cup
Butter, honey, or marmalade   topping

Combine flour, baking powder, and salt in a bowl. Cut in butter with a pastry blender or 2 knives. Mix together currants, ½ cup sugar, and egg and stir into dry ingredients. Sprinkle in milk 1 tablespoon at a time. Mix until all ingredients are moist or dough almost cleans side of bowl. Gather dough into a ball. Roll out ½-inch thick on lightly floured board and cut into 2½-inch rounds. Cook on lightly greased griddle or skillet on the stove top about 3 to 5 minutes until golden brown. Turn and cook on other side until cake is set and roll in sugar. Makes 5 dozen.

Barabrith   (Raisin Bread)

Yeast   1 tablespoon
Warm water   ¼ cup
Sugar   1 cup
Flour   6 to 6¼ cups
Eggs   2
Milk   2 cups scalded
Butter   ¼ cup
Cloves   1 teaspoon
Allspice   1 teaspoon
Cinnamon   1 teaspoon
Candied pineapple   1 cup
Salt   1 teaspoon
Currants   1 cup

Dissolve yeast in water. Add sugar, 2 cups flour, and eggs. Mix well and let sit 30 minutes. To milk add remaining ingredients except flour, then cool. Stir cooled milk mixture into yeast mixture. Add remaining flour and knead well. Let rise to double in bulk. Shape into 4 small loaves and place in greased loaf pans. Let rise to double. Put on trivet on stove top. Cover

with a larger baking pan. Bake about 45 minutes until loaves sound hollow when thumped.
Note: In a conventional oven, bake at 350° for 35 minutes.

Selsig Mor Gannug   (Glamorgan Sausages)

Small onion 1, minced
Fresh bread crumbs 1½ cups
Cheddar cheese ¼ cup grated
Sage pinch
Dry mustard pinch
Salt pinch
Pepper pinch
Water ¼ cup
Egg 1, separated
Flour 2 tablespoons
Dried bread crumbs ½ cup
Shortening 2 tablespoons

Mix first 7 ingredients together. Bind together with water and egg yolk. Shape into sausages. Roll in flour. Beat egg white until frothy. Dip sausage in egg white and roll in dried bread crumbs. Heat a skillet on the stove top and add shortening. When shortening is hot, fry sausages on all sides until lightly browned. Remove from skillet and place in baking dish. Cover dish and set it on a trivet. Cook on stove top another 30 minutes and serve.

Lemon Curd

Butter ½ cup
Sugar 1 cup
Fresh lemon juice 1 cup
Egg yolks 8
Fresh lemon peel 2 tablespoons grated

In a heavy 2-quart saucepan, combine first 4 ingredients. On low heat part of stove, stir mixture until it coats the back of a spoon. Do not boil. Stir in lemon peel. Set on trivet to serve with toast. Refrigerate unused lemon curd to serve on fresh fruit or to use as a tart filling or as a cake topping. Makes 2 cups.

Armenian Supper

Armenians scattered around the world as their own ancient country—site of Mount Ararat and rumored remains of Noah's Ark—dissolved into history because of war, invasion, and conquest. The doors of the United States opened because American missionaries witnessed massacres of some 200,000 people between 1894 and 1896. One group of these homeless people settled in California to grow raisin grapes, as some had done in their homeland.

Although Armenians lost many of their customs to invading cultures and adopted lands, they have shared backgammon and their spicy, unctuous foods with Americans.

One young Armenian couple in California sought to save their ethnic dishes from oblivion when they researched and experimented to develop the old recipes. Then they called their grandmothers in as consultants. Here are some of their results.

To serve this meal, place dishes on trivets on the stove top. Seat guests on a carpet—preferably Persian—in front of the stove. Earthenware dishes and metal mugs add to the Middle Eastern flavor. And bring out the backgammon set. Serves 6.

Marinated Vegetables

Yalanchi Dolmas*   Bulgur Pilaf*
(Stuffed Grape Leaves)

Cheese Halvah*

Spiced Almonds*

Iced Water with Lemon Slices

Yalanchi Dolmas   (Stuffed Grape Leaves)

Corn oil 2 cups
Large onions 6, finely chopped
Stewed tomatoes 16-ounce can
Celery 1 stalk, finely chopped
Green pepper 1, finely chopped
Garlic cloves 2, minced
Ground red pepper dash
Salt to taste
Black pepper to taste
Long grain rice 2 cups
Water 1 cup
Tomato sauce ½ cup
Lemon juice of 1 lemon
Grape leaves 16-ounce jar, rinsed and drained
Water 3 cups
Tomato sauce ½ cup
Lemon juice of 2 or 3 lemons

Heat oil in large skillet. Add onions and cook until transparent. Stir in next 7 ingredients and cook about 5 minutes until blended. Add next 4 ingredients and cook covered about 30 to 60 minutes until all water is absorbed. Remove from heat and chill. When ready to assemble, place 1 tablespoon filling in each grape leaf, vein side up, and roll tightly. Arrange close together in a Dutch oven or large heavy saucepan. Add remaining water, tomato sauce, and lemon juice and cover with a layer of grape leaves. Place a heavy plate over the grape leaf rolls. Set pan or Dutch oven on trivet on stove top and let simmer about 30 minutes until liquid is absorbed. For a tarter flavor add more lemon juice. Serve chilled. Makes 100 appetizers.

Note: The filling for the leaves can be made the night before on the evening fire.

Bulgur Pilaf

Shortening   2 tablespoons
Coil-style vermicelli   ½ cup crushed
Butter   ¼ cup
Onion   1, finely chopped
Green pepper   ¼ cup finely chopped
Coarse bulgur   1 cup
Chicken broth   10½-ounce can, heated
Water
Salt   to taste

Heat shortening in large pan, add vermicelli, and sauté until browned. Add butter and melt. Stir in onion and green pepper and sauté until onion is transparent. Stir in bulgur. Add enough water to broth to make 2 cups. Gradually stir liquids into bulgur. Simmer until liquid is absorbed. Add salt and remove to a trivet on low heat part of stove. Serves 6.

Cheese Halvah

Sugar   2 cups
Water   2 cups
Butter   1 cup
Flour   2½ cups
Monterey Jack cheese   ½ pound, grated
Cinnamon
Slivered almonds

Combine sugar and water in saucepan and boil until syrupy. Put skillet on stove top and melt butter. With a wooden spoon, stir in flour until brown and smooth. Alternately stir in cheese and sugar water, finishing with liquid. When halvah is a pliable consistency, press into a 9-inch pie plate. Turn onto a platter and place on trivet over low heat part of stove. Sprinkle with cinnamon and press almonds into top. Serve warm. Refrigerate unused portion for later use.

Spiced Almonds

Confectioners' sugar 1¼ cups
Salt 1 teaspoon
Ginger 1 teaspoon
Cinnamon ¼ teaspoon
Nutmeg ½ teaspoon
Cloves ½ teaspoon
Water 1 tablespoon
Egg white 1
Almonds ½ pound shelled, blanched, and dried

Mix first 6 ingredients and divide into 2 portions. Add water to egg white and beat slightly. Coat almonds with egg white mixture by dipping while they are in a slotted spoon or coarse strainer. Roll in 1 portion of spiced sugar. In a shallow baking pan, layer 1 portion of spiced sugar, then nuts, and then other portion of sugar on top. Place on trivet on low heat part of stove and let roast 2 to 3 hours, stirring occasionally. Nuts will be covered with thin brittle coating when done.

Spanish-American Mission Meal

Spanish Catholic missionaries sailed to southwestern North America in 1769 about the time the thirteen colonies were brewing tea in Boston Harbor. The Spanish, with their grape cuttings and fruit-tree seedlings, started California's vineyards and orchards and introduced the natives to fruits as well as beef. The Spanish, Indians, and Mexicans "potlucked" it and served up "mission" cooking.

Simple white linen, plain china, and a dried flower arrangement in a pottery bowl enhance the table for this meal. Serves 6.

Spanish Steak*

Stuffed Peppers*

Maiz Caliente sobre Tomatoes y Cebollas*
(Hot Corn on Tomatoes and Onion)

Sourdough Bread

Lemon Pudding*
or
Peach Pudding*

*Mexican Chocolate**

Spanish Steak

Beef round steak 2 pounds, cut in 6 pieces
Flour ¼ cup
Oil 2 tablespoons
Tomatoes 16-ounce can
Kidney beans 15½-ounce can, drained
Green pepper ¼ cup chopped
Vinegar 2 tablespoons
Sugar 1 tablespoon
Salt 1 teaspoon
Chili powder 1 teaspoon
Cumin ½ teaspoon

Tenderize meat with meat pounder and pound in flour. In a skillet, heat oil and brown meat on both sides. Combine remaining ingredients and pour over steak. Place on stove top and cover. Simmer about an hour until meat is tender.

Stuffed Peppers

Ground beef 1 pound
Water 3 cups
Tomatoes 16-ounce can
Cornmeal 1 cup
Vinegar 2 tablespoons
Worcestershire sauce 2 teaspoons
Salt and pepper to taste
Butter 1 tablespoon
Green peppers 10
Salt 1 tablespoon

Combine meat and water in saucepan and cook until meat is done. Add remaining ingredients. Slice 1 end off each pepper and remove seeds and membranes. Parboil with 1 tablespoon salt. Drain and cool. Fill with meat mixture and place in 2-quart casserole with cover. Cover and put on trivet on stove top and cook until meat mixture in pepper is done.
Note: In a conventional oven, bake at 350° for 30 minutes.

Maiz Caliente sobre Tomatoes y Cebollas
(Hot Corn on Tomatoes and Onion)

Oil ½ cup
Onions 1½ cups minced
Whole kernel corn   three 12-ounce cans
Salt 2½ teaspoons
Pepper ½ teaspoon
Tomatoes 3 cups diced
Lemon juice 5 teaspoons
Cayenne dash

Heat oil in saucepan and sauté ½ cup onion until soft. Add corn, ½ teaspoon salt, and ¼ teaspoon pepper. Stir well. Cover pan and let cook slowly about 30 minutes. In a serving dish combine tomatoes, remaining 1 cup onion, 2 teaspoons salt, ¼ teaspoon pepper, lemon juice, and cayenne. Pour hot corn mixture over this and serve.

Lemon Pudding

Egg whites 2
Salt ¼ teaspoon
Sugar ½ cup
Egg yolks 2
Lemon zest 1 tablespoon grated
Lemon juice 2 teaspoons
Butter 2 teaspoons, melted
Sugar ½ cup
Flour 3 tablespoons
Milk 1 cup

Beat egg whites and salt until stiff. Add ½ cup sugar. Beat together next 4 ingredients. Mix ½ cup sugar and flour and stir into egg yolk mixture. Add milk, then fold in egg white mixture. Pour into 1½-quart baking dish, cover with foil, and tie with string. Set on rack in large steamer kettle and add ½-inch hot water. Cover pan and cook about 1 hour until pudding is set and knife comes out clean.
Note: In a conventional oven, bake at 350° for 50 to 60 minutes.

Peach Pudding

Flour 2 cups sifted
Salt ½ teaspoon
Baking powder 4 teaspoons
Shortening 2 tablespoons
Milk 1 cup
Peaches 3 cups sliced
Whipped cream or butterscotch sauce topping

Sift together flour, salt, and baking powder. Cut in shortening with 2 knives or pastry blender. Stir in milk to make soft dough. Put peaches in greased baking dish and spread dough over fruit. Set dish on rack in steamer kettle with ½ inch of water boiling in it. Cover kettle tightly. Steam about an hour until dough is done. Invert pudding onto serving platter and serve with whipped cream. Serves 8 to 10.

Mexican Chocolate

Milk 6 cups
Cinnamon ¼ teaspoon
Semisweet chocolate 6 ounces, coarsely chopped
Whipping cream ½ cup, whipped
Sugar 2 tablespoons
Whole cinnamon sticks 6
Whipped cream garnish

Heat milk with cinnamon. Add chocolate, stir until melted, then beat until frothy. Whip cream with sugar. Drop a stick of cinnamon in each cup, then pour in chocolate. Top with whipped cream.

Tyrolean Christmas

Over a million fugitives fled the Tyrolean region of the European Alps when Adolph Hitler seized Austria in 1938. Among some 200,000 who came to the United States was the Baroness Maria Augusta von Trapp and her singing family, who settled in Stowe, Vermont. During the twelve days of Christmas Tyroleans would relive their traditional festival with singing and feasting on roast goose, along with other dishes acquired from the frugal and charming Vermont Yankees of the snowy, land-locked mountains that were so like those at home.

After caroling your neighbors, return to the warmth of home and savor this sumptuous meal. Serves 6.

Almond Milk*

Roast Goose*

Creamed Celery*   Glazed Beets*

Stewed Apples*

Fruit Cake

Salzburger Nockerl*

Strong Coffee with Sweetened Whipped Cream

Almond Milk

Water 2 cups
Almonds 12, finely chopped
Sugar 3 tablespoons
Orange juice ¼ cup

Place water and almonds in a saucepan. Let sit until mixture looks like milk. Put water and almonds in a blender and pulverize. Strain mixture through cheesecloth. Return to pan with sugar and orange juice. Heat through and serve warm.

Roast Goose

Chestnuts 1 cup roasted
Salt
Salt 1 teaspoon
Marjoram ½ teaspoon
Pepper ¼ teaspoon
Goose 1, dressed
Water 1 cup
Stock (see Index) 1 cup

Peel, mash, and lightly salt chestnuts. Mix together 1 teaspoon salt, marjoram and pepper and rub over goose. Stuff cavity in goose breast with chestnuts. Place goose on rack in roasting pan and pour in water and stock. Cover pan and cook until goose leg pulls from body. Baste with water and stock throughout cooking.

Creamed Celery

Butter 2 tablespoons
Onion 1 tablespoon minced
Celery best stalks of 2 heads, cut in ½-inch pieces
Hot water ½ cup
Heavy cream ½ cup
Nutmeg pinch
Sherry 1 tablespoon
Egg yolks 2

Melt butter in a large skillet. Add onion and celery and toss to coat. Add water and simmer vegetables until tender. When most of the water has been reduced in the pan, add cream and nutmeg and heat through. Beat sherry and eggs with fork. Pour a little of the hot cream into the eggs and stir well. Add egg mixture to celery in pan. Cook slowly until thick, stirring to keep ingredients blended. Serve hot from the stove top.

Glazed Beets

Beets 2 cups
Water
Quick tapioca 1 tablespoon
Lemon juice 2 tablespoons
Burgundy wine 2 tablespoons
Sugar 1 teaspoon
Salt and pepper to taste

Cook beets in water until tender, then drain, reserving 1 cup juice. Soak tapioca in beet juice for 5 minutes. Add remaining ingredients and bring to simmer on stove top. Cook until mixture thickens, stirring to make smooth sauce. Pour over beets and serve hot from stove top.

Stewed Apples

Large Rome apples* 3, sliced
Cinnamon 1 stick
Whole cloves 4
Brown sugar ½ cup

Put all ingredients into a pot with a cover. Set on stove top and let simmer until apples are cooked through. Remove cinnamon and cloves before serving.

* Or other cooking apple.

Salzburger Nockerl

Egg yolks 10
Sugar ¼ cup
Egg whites 10, beaten until stiff
Flour 5 tablespoons
Milk ¾ cup
Butter 4 tablespoons
Confectioners' sugar

This recipe requires your undivided attention. Beat egg yolks in mixing bowl with sugar until yolks are creamy. Blend in egg whites and flour. Heat milk and butter in a flat pan. Very slowly add egg and sugar mixture to the hot milk. Cook together until mixture is slightly thickened. Cover pan, place on a trivet on the stove top, and let mixture set. Sift confectioners' sugar over the top of the pan while hot and just before serving.

Hawaiian Luau

    Bask in the warmth of your wood stove and dream of warm waves and Hawaiian sunshine while you enjoy a luau. Traditionally, Hawaiians blend dishes from a composite of peoples—Japanese, Filipinos, Chinese, original Hawaiians, Puerto Ricans, Portuguese, and Caucasians of mixed nationalities. For this occasion, you can cover the table with fishnets or woven bamboo and use a centerpiece of fruit, flowers, and ferns. You can shed your shoes in the Japanese mode and eat sans silverware, if you desire. All will be appropriately American because, after twenty-two attempts, the islands of Hawaii became our fiftieth state in 1959, bringing us tropical sunshine, sandy island beaches, luaus, and a potpourri of cultures.
    While indulging in the feast, heed the words of an old Hawaiian chief: "Look not with ungracious eyes upon the traveler who passes your door. You must bid him enter. Your pig must be killed. Whoever does not respect this order is to be taken to the public place and shamed." Serves 6.

Japanese Clear Soup*

Shrimp Curry*   Rice

Roast Loin of Pork*

Potato-Pineapple Salad*   Luau Green Beans*

Baked Bananas*

Kona Coffee

Japanese Clear Soup

Seaweed 3-inch piece, dried
Bonita* ½ cup flaked and dried
Boiling water 5 cups
Seasoning salt ¼ teaspoon
Soy sauce ½ teaspoon
Salt 1 teaspoon
White pepper dash
Turnip sliced diagonally, garnish
Carrot sliced diagonally, garnish

In a saucepan, boil together the seaweed and fish in water. Move pan to a low heat part of stove and let fish settle. Strain liquid and add next 4 ingredients. Serve garnished with turnip and carrot.
* Or use any dried mackerel-type fish.

Shrimp Curry

Boiling water 1 cup
Coconut meat of 1, grated
Butter 3 tablespoons
Onion ½ cup minced
Flour 3 tablespoons
Curry powder 1 tablespoon
Salt 1 teaspoon
Sugar ½ teaspoon
Ground ginger ½ teaspoon
Milk 2 cups
Shrimp 3 cups
Rice 3 cups cooked
Bacon ½ pound, fried and crumbled
Coconut 1 cup grated
Peanuts 1 cup chopped
Eggs 2, hard-cooked and chopped
Onions ½ cup minced
Macadamia nuts 1 cup chopped

Pour water over coconut and let stand until cool. Drain, saving liquid. Melt butter in skillet and sauté onion. Stir in next 5 ingredients. Gradually stir in milk and liquid drained from coconut. Stir in shrimp and heat through. Serve over rice, with remaining ingredients as garnishes.
* Or you can use lobster, crab, or chicken.

Roast Loin of Pork

Lean pork roast 3½ pounds
Crystallized ginger 2 tablespoons finely chopped
Soy sauce ¼ cup
Watercress (optional)

Make slits all over roast. Insert 1 tablespoon ginger in slits. Combine rest of ginger with soy sauce. Brush over roast. Place meat on rack in a Dutch oven. Place on stove top and let cook until meat temperature reaches 185°F. Garnish with watercress if desired.
Note: In a conventional oven, cook at 325° for 1 hour and 45 minutes.

Potato-Pineapple Salad

Potatoes 4 cups cooked and diced
Fresh pineapple 2 cups crushed or
   Canned crushed pineapple 20-ounce can
Onion ¼ cup minced
Cooked Salad Dressing ¼ cup
Salt 1 teaspoon

Cook potatoes a day ahead. The next day, combine potatoes with other ingredients. Toss together and serve.

Cooked Salad Dressing

Sugar 3 tablespoons
Salt 1 teaspoon
Prepared mustard 1 teaspoon
Flour 1½ tablespoons
Egg 1
Milk ¾ cup
Vinegar ¼ cup
Butter 1 teaspoon
Mayonnaise ¼ to ½ cup

In a saucepan combine all ingredients except butter and mayonnaise. Put on stove top and stir constantly until mixture thickens. Stir in butter and mayonnaise. Use on any potato salad, macaroni salad, or coleslaw.

Luau Green Beans

French-style green beans 2 cups
Water
Butter 2 tablespoons
Soya sauce ¼ cup

Simmer beans in water until tender. Just before serving, toss lightly with butter and soya sauce. Simmer to heat through and serve from stove top.

Baked Bananas

Medium bananas 6 to 8, firm
Orange 1, peeled and cut in chunks
Orange juice 2 tablespoons
Lemon juice 2 tablespoons
Brown sugar ⅓ cup
Cinnamon dash
Nutmeg dash

Peel bananas and arrange with orange in 1½-quart casserole dish. Mix together remaining ingredients and pour over bananas. Cover casserole and set on trivet on stove top. Let cook until liquid becomes syrupy. Serve hot from stove top.
Note: On a conventional stove, cook at 325° for 25 minutes.

Stove Care

1. The first firing of a new stove can permanently etch the iron or stain the enamel with an acid that condenses on the surface. To avoid this, prop the lid or door of the stove slightly open the first time you light up. Stand by to wipe off the condensate as it appears. Once the stove has heated through, this will not happen.
2. Use proper tools on the stove. A poker is a single length of iron, hooked at the end, that is used to push logs into place, stir coals, and adjust dampers when handles are too hot to touch. Tongs are used to lift big burning logs. A small fine brush broom sweeps away ashes.
3. Do not use the stove as a trash incinerator or fill it with softwood kindling while both drafts and the door are open. The stove will turn red hot.
4. Avoid sudden temperature changes. Do not throw cold water on a hot stove or the stove may crack.
5. Never use kerosene, gasoline, or charcoal to start a fire.
6. Check all dampers and vent controls for proper functioning at least once a year and treat them with a greaseless spray lubricant.
7. Thoroughly clean the stove after each heating season, or more often depending on how much it is used. Use a wire brush to remove ashes, soot, and grime from the interior.
8. Check the exterior for cracks and loose joints. Seal any cracks with a paste made from equal amounts of ashes and common salt mixed with water until it is a workable consistency. Fill cracks when the stove is hot or cold. Tighten joints.
9. Clean bad rust spots on cast iron with coarse salt or commercial rust remover. Then coat the stove with stove blacking, which has a high carbon content and comes in paste, solid, or liquid form. (Or make your own from one part powdered graphite and two parts boiled linseed oil.) Apply to a cold stove with a soft cloth and buff to a bright finish with a dry cloth. If you want to do a more extensive job, paint the stove with flameproof black paint.

Creosote

Creosote will build up in stovepipes and chimneys no matter how careful you are. The sticky tar collects where hot air meets cold air, and is highly flammable. To minimize buildups, take these precautions:

1. Choose a stove of the proper size for the area you want to heat. A stove that is too large for the space will operate with closed drafts most of the time and so will not get hot enough to burn off creosote deposits.
2. Burn only seasoned, dry wood.

3. Regulate drafts to keep a good flow of air through the stove and chimney. Routinely open the door and flues completely to burn off creosote. (Do not do this for more than fifteen minutes on stoves with automatic thermostats.)
4. Clean chimneys routinely every summer and check at regular intervals throughout the season. Watch for chimney fires in the fall when you start the first fires.
5. To clean your own chimney, hire a chimney sweep, or have him come once so you can study his technique and ask questions. Then buy your own brushes and clean routinely.
6. Be careful not to damage the chimney with your cleaning techniques. Some sweeps frown on chemical cleaning substances, which just give you a salty fire and corrode stoves and pipes.
7. Allow yourself the luxury of installing a self-cleaning insulated chimney. It is a highly insulated construction of fire brick, vermiculite, and common brick.

Ashes

Ashes are a reality of wood stoves. They can be an asset as well. These tips should help.
1. Excess ash buildup hampers the air flow. Depending on how often you use the stove, you should remove ashes every three to five days.
2. Use a small shovel or special stove rake to remove ashes.
3. To protect the floor and bottom plate from extreme heat and prolong your stove's life, leave about an inch of ashes in the stove.
4. Before removing the ashes, use them for cooking.
5. Ashes can still hold enough heat to cause a fire after being removed from the stove if they are stored in an enclosed space.
6. Cover stored ashes to avoid leaching of useful elements.
7. Use ashes on your garden to discourage slugs and to add potash and other nutrients to the soil, or on your compost heap to discourage rats and mice. Or use them to make soap (see the "Soap Making" section). Sprinkle them on icy paths and sidewalks.

Ten Wood Tips

1. Ask the following questions if you buy wood: Is it hard or soft? Does it measure a full cord—four by four by eight feet? Does it have insect damage? When was it cut? Is it dry or green and priced accordingly? Does the price include delivery?
2. Cut wood in fall and winter when sap is low.
3. Season wood six to eighteen months depending on the weather in your area.
4. Crisscross the wood, one foot off the ground, as you stack it. Cover it for faster drying. To test for dryness, try to break a kindling-sized stick across your knee. If the wood bends, it is not dry.
5. Scavenge discarded wood from such places as mills, factories, and dumps, and from national forest land, where wood cutting is allowed by permit. Prunings from fruit trees and your own landscape trees are suitable firewood.
6. Compressed logs made from waste wood are safe only if specified for wood stoves. (Aglo Fuel Log by Agnew Environmental Products of Grants Pass, Oregon, contains no additives and is safe to use.)
7. Softwoods provide quick-starting, high-heat fires. Hardwoods provide longer lasting, steady fires. (Refer also to "Heat Value of Woods.")
8. For kindling, use dry softwood split into small pieces.
9. Use the most dense wood available.
10. The old-timers' method of burning greenwood proportionately with hardwood does not prevent creosote buildup or serve any other good purpose.

Heat Value of Woods

Species	Type of Wood	Heat Per Cord (Million BTU)	Amount of Heat
Alder	Hard	11	Low
Apple*	Fruit	27	High
Ash*	Hard	23	High
Avocado	Fruit	15	Low
Beech*	Hard	27	High
Birch, yellow*	Hard	27	High
Cherry*	Fruit	20	Medium
Chestnut	Hard	18	Medium
Dogwood*	Hard	27	High
Fir, Douglas	Soft	18	Medium
Fir, true	Soft	16	Medium
Hemlock	Soft	15	Medium
Hickory*	Hard	27	High
Maple	Hard	23.6	Medium
Oak*	Hard	27	High
Pecan*	Hard	26	High
Pine	Soft	15	Low
Poplar	Hard	15	Low

* Best woods for cooking

Smoke	Coaling Quality	Comments
Low	Fair	
Low	Excellent	Aromatic
Low	Good	
Low	Poor	
Low	Good	Excellent
Low	Good	Moderate sparking
Low	Excellent	
Medium	Fair	Poor overall
Low	Good	Excellent
Heavy	Fair	Available only in West
Medium	Fair	Good kindling
Medium	Poor	
None	Excellent	Excellent overall
Low	Good	
None	Excellent	Excellent overall
None	Good	Available only in South
Medium	Poor	Fair logs, good kindling
Medium	Poor	Poor overall

Safe Temperatures for Meat and Poultry

Meat and Poultry	Internal Temperature
Beef	
Extra rare	120° F
Rare	140° F
Medium	160° F
Well	170° F
Lamb	
Medium	170° F
Well	180° F
Pork	
Safe	137° F
Fresh	170 to 185° F
Cured (labeled "Cook before eating")	160° F
Cured (labeled "Picnic")	170° F
Fully cooked or cured	130° F (heated to enhance flavor)
Veal	
Well	170° F
Chicken	
Done	180 to 185° F in inner thigh (or when thigh pulls easily from body)
Turkey	
Done	180 to 185° F (or when pulls from leg or breastbone)
Done, with stuffing	165° F
Boneless roast	170 to 175° F

Index

Accessories for stoves, 19–20
Appetizers
  Apricot Fondue, 201
  Deviled Crab, 199
  Eggplant Appetizer, 200
  Glamorgan Sausages, 217
  Hot Clam Dip, 199
  Hot Tangy Tomato Juice, 200
  Mushrooms Divine, 199
  Queso, 202
  Selsig Mor Gannug, 217
  Stuffed Grape Leaves, 219
  Yalanchi Dolmas, 219
Ashes, 13, 234

Bacon Gravy, 98
Beverages
  Almond Milk, 226
  "Boiled" Coffee, 53
  Chocolate Drink, 54
  Coffee, 201
  Hot Buttered Rum, 55
  Mulled Cider, 54
  Mulled Wine, 55
  Strong Tea, 215
Biscuits
  "Army Biscuits," 146
  Sourdough Biscuits, 146
Breads
  Barabrith, 216
  Boston Brown Bread, 136
  Corn Bread
    Ash Cakes, 140
    Corn Bread, 138
    Mennonite Corn Bread, 139
    "Pot Likker" Corn Bread, 141
    Smoky Mountain Corn Bread, 140
    Spoon Bread, 142
  Corn-Pumpkin Bread, 213
  Crullers, 150
  Danish Aebleskiver, 148
  George Washington's Hoecakes, 142
  Halloween Bread, 151
  Kansas Corn Cake, 138
  Lefse, 152
  Oat Bread, 137
  Pancake Balls, 148
  Pulla Coffee Bread, 196
  Raisin Bread, 216
  Sheepherder's Bread, 210
  War Brown Bread, 136
  Yeast Sally Lunn, 143

Cakes
  Beer Cake, 184
  Booze Cakes, 185
  Captain's Cake, 183
  Fig Butter Cake, 197
  Gingerbread-Applesauce Pudding Cake, 158
  Great Grandma's Carrot Cake, 179
  Kermakakku, 197
  Seed Cake, 182
  Sour Cream Cake, 197
  Viikunakakku, 197
  War Cake, 181
Chimney cleaning, 233–34
Cookware, 11–13, 16–18
Creosote, 13, 233–34

Desserts. *See* Sweets
Dumplings
  Blackberry Dumplings, 177
  Oregon Trail Plum Dumplings, 176
  Potato Dumplings, 149
  Prune Dumplings, 175
  Shaker Apple Dumplings, 173

Fire, 13, 19–20   *See also* Wood.

Main Dishes
  Beef
    American Roast Beef, 74
    Barbecued Short Ribs, 203
    Beef and Potatoes, 75
    Beef Stew, 80
    Bewitched Liver, 91
    Chili Con Carne, 81
    Chinese Steamed Buns, 88
    Corned Beef, 90
    Cornish Pasties, 77
    Cranberry Meatballs, 85
    Creole Liver, 92
    Four-Layered Dinner, 76
    Grillades, 80
    Hamburger and Corn Hot Dish, 87
    Hum Bow, 88
    Kreplach, 86
    Lengua-con-Setas, 209
    Mount Vernon Baked Short Ribs, 88
    Old Country Cabbage Balls, 83
    Paste, 103
    Pickled Tongue, 92
    Polenta, 84
    Range Stew, 76
    Red Flannel Hash, 89
    Sauerbraten, 73
    Skipperlabskava, 75
    Sour Pot Roast, 73
    Spanish Steak, 222
    Stew with Dumplings, 78

Stuffed Peppers, 223
Swedish Glottstek, 74
Swedish Meatballs, 86
Swiss Steak, 79
Tamales, 204
Texas Chili, 82
Tongue with Mushroom Sauce, 209
Lamb
   Irish Lamb Stew, 93
   Moussaka à la Grecque, 94
Meatless
   Barley-Mushroom Casserole, 133
   Cheese Fondue, 130
   Cheese-Herb Frittata, 131
   Corn Oysters, 132
   Cornmeal Mush, 132
   Filbert Pie, 129
   Queso, 202
   Russian Mushrooms, 134
   Welsh Rabbit, 130
Pork
   Bacon Gravy, 98
   Beer-Glazed Sausages, 105
   Boiled Ham, 102
   Colonial Pork Chops, 96
   Country Kraut, 104
   Cowboy Stew, 99
   Feast Day Pork Roast, 212
   Hoppin John, 101
   La Garbure, 208
   Lentils with Polish Sausage, 104
   Pork Chops with Brown Rice, 95
   Pork Roast, 194
   Posole, 98
   Red Beans and Rice, 100
   Roast Loin of Pork, 231
   Sauterne Pork Chops, 96
   Schnitz und Knepp, 102
   Stew, 208
   Sweet and Sour Pork, 97
Poultry
   Barbecued Chicken, 203
   Braised Duck, 112
   Chicken and Caraway Seeds, 114
   Chicken and Dumplings, 120
   Chicken and Mushrooms, 119
   Chicken Fricassee, 117
   Country Captain, 118
   Danish Chicken, 115
   Duck in Sake Sauce, 112
   Festive Turkey, 110
   Kamo Yoshino-Ni, 112
   Kylling Med Karve, 114
   Mission Chicken, 116
   Paella, 121
   Pigeon with Peas, 109
   Randolph-Macon Chicken Deluxe, 114
   Roast Goose, 226
   Saucy Apple Goose, 113
   Smothered Pheasant, 109
   Threshers' Chicken Casserole, 116
Rabbit
   Rabbit Oswego, 108
   Rabbit Pot au Feu, 107
   Swiss Rabbit, 108
Seafood
   Arrosa Chirlagas eta Peregilgas, 209
   Bacalado-con-Pimiento, 208
   Baked Trout with Sour Cream, 128
   Brook Trout with Chablis and Dill, 127
   Codfish with Pimientos, 208
   Hangtown Fry, 124
   Maryland Crab Cakes, 124
   Norwegian Salmon Pudding, 126
   Paella, 121
   Pine-Bark Fish Stew, 128
   Poached Salmon, 126
   Rice and Clams, 209
   Salmon in Ashes, 125
   Shrimp Curry, 230
   "Too Stew Oystors," 123
   Wickford Quahog Pie, 122
Veal
   Veal Loaf, 90
Venison
   Braised Venison, 106
   Hunter's Stew, 107
Meat, safe temperatures for, 238
Muffins
   English Muffins, 145

Pancakes
   Danish Aebleskiver, 148
   Pancake Balls, 148
   Sourdough Pancakes, 148
Parties
   Armenian Supper, 218
   Basque Boardinghouse Spread, 207
   Finnish Wood Gathering Party, 193
   Hawaiian Luau, 229
   Pueblo-Navajo Feast, 211
   Southern Cocktail Party, 198
   Spanish-American Mission Meal, 222
   Tex-Mex Barbecue, 202
   Tyrolean Christmas, 225
   Welsh Tea, 215
Poultry, safe temperatures for, 238
Puddings
   Apricot-Rice Pudding, 214
   Blueberry Steamed Pudding, 164
   Carrot Pudding, 167
   Chocolate Pudding, 170
   Cinnamon Pudding, 159
   Cranberry Pudding, 162
   Date Pudding, 164
   Indiana Persimmon Pudding, 161

Indian Pudding, 166
Lemon Pudding, 224
Maple Bread Pudding, 169
Original Indian Pudding, 165
Peach Pudding, 224
Plum Pudding, 163
Rice Pudding, 160
Roly-Poly Pudding, 168

Sauce
Custard Sauce, 168
Italian Sauce, 84
Salsa Jalapeño, 204

Scones
Griddle Scones, 144

Side Dishes
Apple-Stuffed Acorn Squash, 60
Barley and Pine Nut Casserole, 59
Boston Baked Beans, 70
Bulgar Pilaf, 220
Chestnut Puree, 60
Corn Pudding, 64
Cowpoke Beans, 69
Creamed Celery, 227
Frijoles Refritos, 205
Glazed Beets, 227
"Green Steak," 67
Gruyère Cheese Grits, 68
Hot Corn on Tomatoes and Onion, 223
Hot German Potato Salad, 64
Hot Squash Salad, 195
Luau Green Beans, 232
Maiz Caliente sobre Tomatoes y Cebollas, 223
Maple Baked Beans, 71
Pennsylvania Red Cabbage, 66
Pine Nut Pilaf, 58
Plain Grits, 68
Pompion Pye, 61
Potato Casserole, 195
Potatoes and Pineapple, 63
Potato-Pineapple Salad, 231
Rice Apples, 57
Risotto à la Milanèse, 58
San Fernando Beans, 70
Shaker Spinach, 66
Snaps with an "Old Ham Bone," 65
Succotash, 213
Sweet Potato Casserole, 62
Sweet Potato Pudding, 62
Yams with Apples, 62

Soups
Baked Bean Soup, 40
Bean Soup, 40
Beef Stock, 29
Bouillon, 31
Brunswick Stew, 34
Chicken Stock, 30
Cioppino, 37
Consommé, 32
Corn Chowder, 45
Depression Stew, 41
Dutch Corn Soup, 46
Fish Stock, 30
Fruit Soup, 52
German Lentil Soup, 42
Greens Soup, 50
Japanese Clear Soup, 230
Lamb-Cabbage Soup, 32
Mandu, 35
Mushroom Soup, 51
Oyster Stew, 39
Potage Crécy, 49
Potato-Leek Chowder, 47
Puerto Rican Soup, 36
Puree of Carrot Soup, 49
Scotch Broth, 33
Seafood Gumbo, 38
Split Pea Soup, 44
Stocks, 29
Summer Squash Soup, 212
Swedish Pea Soup, 43
Tomato Soup, 48
Vegetable Soup, 52
Vegetable Stock, 31
Virginia Peanut Soup, 44

Sourdough Starter, 147

Stoves: care of, 233–34; history of, 9–11; methods of cooking on, 20–26. *See also* Accessories for stoves

Sweets
Applachian Apple Butter, 191
Apple Charlotte, 158
Apple Compote, 155
Apple Custard, 154
Apple Date Dream, 180
Apple Pandowdy, 171
Baked Bananas, 232
Blueberry Cobbler, 172
Brown Sugar Shortbread, 188
Cheesecake, 186
Cheese Halvah, 220
Cherry Michel, 156
Date Candy, 190
Dried Apple Duff, 178
Dutch-Oven Gingerbread, 157
Flana, 210
Gingerbread, 156
Green-Tomato Mincemeat Turnovers, 174
Griddle Cookies, 186
Huckle Buckle, 178
Lemon Curd, 217
Lemon Custard, 154
Lemon Pot Pie, 172

Index

Mexican Chocolate, 225
Peanut Butter Candy, 190
Pears in Red Wine, 210
Pineapple Nugget Cookies, 187
Pralines, 206
Rhubarb Conserve, 190
Salzburger Nockerl, 228
Spiced Almonds, 221
Stewed Apples, 228
Taffy Creams, 189
Tea Cookies, 188
Teisen Cymraeg, 216
Welsh Cakes, 216
See also Cakes; Dumplings; Puddings

Teakettles, 17–18

Utensils, 15–18

Wood, 19, 236–37